Pete Napolitano began his career in the produce industry in the early 1950s at the tender age of five, peddling fruit and vegetables door-to-door to help support his family's New Jersey-based produce business. "Discovered" at his store by a TV producer decades later and given the moniker "Produce Pete," he's since become a fixture on WNBC's *Weekend Today in New York* show, where his tips on selecting, storing, and preparing various produce items – all shared in his authentic, endearing, and plain-speaking style – have captivated viewers in metro New York and other U.S. and international markets for 30 years and rendered him one of the longest-running segments in TV history.

In *They Call Me Produce Pete,* Napolitano shares candid memories of growing up poor in post-WWII America, striving to achieve the American Dream, and landing unexpected fame as one of the nation's leading experts on produce. Sprinkled with touching stories, photos, and family recipes that have held a special place in his heart throughout his life, *They Call me Produce Pete* is a nostalgic nod to simpler times and a must-read for anyone who dares to dream the impossible.

Hardcover ISBN- 9798986988306
Paperback ISBN- 9798986988313
eBook ISBN- 9798986988320

Published in the United States of America
Printed in the United States of America

Table of Contents

Index of Recipes

"Produce Pete" Napolitano as a young boy, making change for customers at Frankie's Market in Lodi, NJ (rendering by Kurt Otto)

A Note to Readers from "Produce Pete" Napolitano

Without the love and support of my lifetime partner and wife, Bette, this book and my life wouldn't be complete. I have to thank my mom and dad, who, even though things were tough growing up, always made a home for us. I of course have to thank my family, friends, fans, and my WNBC family for making my life complete. And last but not least, I have to thank Susan Bloom, who became "me" during the writing of this book and without whom this book would never have happened.

They say hard work will never kill you and I guess that proved to be true in my life; nothing came easy to me, but I've realized that all of the experiences we have – good and bad – are what make us who we are. In that sense, my life has been blessed. Memories and food, food and memories – it's what my life is all about.

Wishing you and your family health, happiness, and indelible memories of your own. Enjoy –

Pete

The World According to Produce Pete

Pete's old stomping grounds growing up in the produce business in northern New Jersey

Prologue

The sun is just coming up as I drive across the George Washington Bridge and head into the WNBC-TV studios in New York City (pre-pandemic). It's a drive that I've made every Saturday morning for the last 30 years in order to do my weekly 'Produce Pete' segment on WNBC 4 New York's *Weekend Today in New York* morning show and one that I've come to know well – though at the same time an incredible opportunity that I could never have imagined would be a reality when I was growing up in North Jersey as the oldest son of an immigrant produce peddler.

My routine, at least for the last several years up until the pandemic, has gone like this. On the Tuesday or Wednesday before each Saturday morning's broadcast, I e-mail our show's producer to confirm the exact fruit or vegetable I'm going to cover on that Saturday's show. I like to wait until the last minute to do that to ensure the quality and availability of the item – two musts for me – because I don't want to talk about something that viewers can't find in their local store; for that reason, you'll never see me covering something like cherries in January. I then send the producer an outline of the information I'm going to share in my segment so that the team can prepare highlights to include on the ticker or 'crawl line' running on the bottom of the TV screen during the segment.

On the Wednesday before the Saturday show, I usually buy several cases of the product I'm going to be talking about. Though I'm sure a number of providers would be happy to supply me with free produce for use on the show in exchange for a mention, I've never taken products for free from anyone for the segment and have always bought my own products outright to ensure that there are no conflicts of interest and that I'm able to share my opinions on produce free and clear each week – another must for me. On Thursday, the producer gets back to me with the approximate time that my segment will be airing that Saturday and who will be on the crew.

When Saturday morning rolls around, I get up at around 3 a.m. (my usual wake-up hour after a lifetime in the produce business), get ready to go, and post a note to Twitter, Facebook, and Instagram by 5 a.m. about what I'll be discussing on the show that morning and which anchors will be joining me, and then leave my house in Passaic County, NJ by around 6:15 or 6:30 a.m. At the point where I cross the George Washington Bridge, I phone the WNBC crew to say that I'll be at the studios in 15 minutes.

Once I arrive at the WNBC studios on 48th Street in Manhattan, a crew member waits for me to carry in the products I've brought and brings them upstairs while I go park. Parking regulations got much tighter at the building after 9/11 and I now use a parking lot across the street. At the WNBC building, security members scan my pass and I get to our studio on the third floor by around 7:30 or 7:45 a.m.

With 60 or 90 minutes to go before my segment, which currently runs at around 9:15 a.m., I go in the back and set up my display. I try to set up my table the same way it would look if I were selling products in my store, showing entire cases of grapefruits or avocados, for example, not just two or three pieces. Depending on the time of year, we may also have props to work into the display as well, such as a Super Bowl tablecloth, heart balloons for Valentine's Day, and/or prepared dishes, like guacamole with chips or chocolate-covered strawberries, which my wife Bette makes the night before.

Discussing the joys of chocolate-covered strawberries with "Weekend Today in New York" news anchor Pat Battle (above) and the features of navel oranges with NBC 4 New York's Jen Maxfield (left) during recent segments of NBC 4 New York's "Weekend Today in New York"

After *Weekend Today in New York's* Raphael Miranda covers the weather forecast, the crew wheels my table out and I do a quick 15-second teaser about what I'll be covering right after the commercial break and why viewers shouldn't miss it. Two minutes later, I'm back on for my segment, which usually runs about 3-5 minutes long and often involves our news anchors, Pat Battle or Gus Rosendale, and/or floor supervisor and ever-ready taste-tester, Tere Mele.

With the "Weekend Today in New York" crew, including (left to right) meteorologist Raphael Miranda and news anchors Pat Battle and Gus Rosendale

When my segment is over at 9:30 a.m., we send all of the produce to the WNBC control room upstairs for distribution to crew members and other colleagues. While the anchors stay on to prepare *Weekend Today in New York* segments that will be aired later in taxis, I get back in my car with any serving pieces I've brought and arrive home by around 11:30. The segment goes up on WNBC's website shortly after – I have my own Produce Pete page (www.nbcnewyork.com/tag/produce-pete/) – and I also post it to my own website (www.producepete.com) as well as to my Twitter, Facebook, and Instagram accounts that afternoon.

I feel honored and privileged to be on WNBC 4 New York every weekend sharing my knowledge from over 70 years of experience in the produce business as "Produce Pete," the version of Pete Napolitano that I've been since my mid-40s. For something I never expected or even wanted to do when I was first offered the chance to be on TV three decades ago, it's totally changed my life and I hope to keep doing the show for another 30 years. I've worked hard to bring viewers the best of my expertise every single week and it's more fun than ever now thanks to the great people I work with and the incredible response I get from our millions of viewers throughout New York, New Jersey, and Connecticut as well as from fans all over the country and the world who have their own WNBC affiliate or who pick up the New York feed.

Among the questions I hear most often, people always want to know how I've lasted this long on TV, a medium well-known for being fast-paced, fickle, and ever-changing. "What's your secret?" they ask. Honestly, I think it's a combination of things. Though I never had any formal training in TV, I was taught to look people in the eye by an Italian immigrant father who came to America knowing no English and having to read facial expressions and non-verbal cues to survive and succeed. I've never been nervous around TV cameras and have considered them like looking into someone's eye.

I also attribute my longevity to honesty, sincerity, consistency, and hard work, all values I learned from both my and Bette's working-class parents and other people I would come to admire and respect throughout my life – people who came from humble beginnings, worked tirelessly to build a better life, and never took an opportunity for granted.

And then there's the food, and the stories. Whether you're the president of the United States, the Queen of England, or a working-class citizen like most of us, everybody eats – and food has an undeniable way of triggering memories. Growing up in a large family with a colorful cast of characters and unforgettable experiences – from incredibly difficult ones to wonderful and special ones – that made an indelible impact on me, I've found that sharing these personal stories during my segments reminds people of simpler times, perhaps similar experiences from their own childhood, and touches viewers in an intangible way that simple hard-and-fast rules on selecting, storing, and preparing produce never could. Though I'm sharing information on produce and recipes, it's the stories and the nostalgia that people love to hear. Maybe that's the real secret to my longevity on TV.

The truth is, how many times has the taste of something brought back all sorts of memories (good or bad)? I can't tell you how often different foods remind me of experiences I've had and people I've known throughout my life. It's all about food and memories, I always say. I hope that the memories and recipes I'm about to share give you a flavor for my story and for the experiences and tastes that have served as the culinary soundtrack of my life.

CHAPTER 1

HUMBLE BEGINNINGS

First, a little bit about how I got here.

I'm a junior – my father, Pietro (Peter) Napolitano, was born on May 30th, 1921 in Campania, Italy, near Naples, and was the youngest of 20 (yes, 20!) children – 17 boys and 3 girls. The youngest three kids (including my pop) went back and forth between Italy and the U.S. a lot and different parts of the family came to the U.S. at different times. Family lore has it that my father was originally placed in a seminary for a planned future as a priest. What I do know for sure was that he and his family lived on Mott Street in New York City's Little Italy when they first arrived in America and then settled at 79 Humphrey Street in Englewood, NJ in the 1930s. He and other family members moved back and forth between New Jersey and Italy in the early years; though Pop lived here until he was six or seven and learned English, he went back to live in Italy until he was 10 or 12 and lost his English language skills. Because he then couldn't speak English when he returned to New Jersey, he was placed in a kindergarten class even though he was at least twice the age of the other kids. I remember him telling me once that his knees hit the top of the small desk-and-chair units that the rest of his pint-size classmates sat in comfortably, which was very embarrassing for him. As it turned out, he ended up dropping out of school entirely after the eighth or ninth grade to work full-time.

Like many immigrants with limited English skills, his parents (my grandparents), Maria and Severio Napolitano, were constantly afraid of being told to leave by the authorities in their newly-adopted country and worked hard to succeed and stay under the radar. Severio held a variety of different jobs, but produce was one of the cheapest businesses you could get into at the time, so produce and food-related ventures became the family trade. Through Maria's family, which had a business that specialized in canned goods, Severio ended up working in canned products like olive oil and tomato sauce. My pop was fairly young when his father died. At that point, all 17 of Severio's sons went in different directions and my father ended up working for his older brothers in their various businesses, which included a butcher shop, a produce operation, and truck driving.

My mother, Louise Grace Morrissey, was born in New York City on March 11th, 1920 to Irish-American parents and was the oldest of four siblings. Though my father's side of the family always referred to her by her given first name, her own family called her Peggy. She graduated from high school in Closter, NJ in 1937 and worked at Woolworth's and eventually A&P in Englewood, which is where she met my father, who was a butcher there. He served in the merchant marines from 1939 to 1941 and then enlisted in World War II from 1941-1945.

My parents got married on March 19th, 1944. Their different religions presented a challenge – Mom was Protestant and Pop was Catholic, which precluded them from being married in a regular church back then – so they married in a seminary. Nonetheless, we kids were raised Catholic and even though my mom never officially changed her religion, we celebrated every Catholic holiday and I used to joke that mom was the best Catholic you'd ever meet; she even taught CCD when my younger sister was going to school.

Mom and Pop in the 1940s

After their wedding, my mom followed Pop down to Camp Shelby in Mississippi and then moved back in with her parents in Tenafly while she awaited his return from wartime service. Pop was involved in the Battle of the Bulge in Belgium in 1944 and other serious military engagements in the Philippines, experiences that would have an indelible impact on his demeanor and approach to life when he returned. Apparently, as the war was ending, soldiers were asked to report to the government any injuries they'd sustained during their time in the service; if you did that, however, they'd keep you in the service longer to treat your injuries, so a lot of soldiers (including Pop) opted not to divulge anything so that they could go home. Several years after his return, he had so much trouble with his back that doctors fused his spine and, as I witnessed all throughout my childhood, he also suffered from a nervous disorder that caused his hands to bleed whenever he was under stress. Family members later confirmed for me that while Pop went into the service a fairly happy fellow, he came home a far more serious and nervous guy and was never the same.

Pop in the Philippines during WWII; family members confirm that he was never the same after he returned

4

I was born on February 23rd, 1945. When my father returned to New Jersey from the service later that year (I was a baby at the time), we moved to Paterson, then Englewood, his hometown.... and then other towns all over Bergen County, NJ, including Ridgefield Park, Paterson again, Tenafly, and Bergenfield. My pop couldn't sit still; even when he retired to Florida years later, he moved four times. I was in a different school every 1-2 years and had to adjust to whole new surroundings and a different set of friends each time. But because we moved around so much, I learned to be social at a very early age, which I think had a lot to do with who I am today.

Pop holding me as a baby in early 1946. He was a
a hard man to love, but I'll love him to the day I die

My brother David was born on November 19th, 1946, 21 months after me, and our family was broke for most of our childhood. Pop held various jobs as a butcher, a bartender, a bus driver for the Red & Tan line, a produce salesman, and other jobs that were so seasonal that it was hard to make ends meet. One time, after Pop lost the bar in Paterson that we lived above and we were left with no place to call home, a good friend of my father's, Pete Oprandy, gave us a house to live in on Serpentine Road in Tenafly which was located right next to a cemetery. It was a rickety old place – I remember my mother actually falling through the floorboards when we first walked in! – but my father was very handy and resourceful, out of necessity. He repaired all of the rotten wood, put up plasterboard, bought the house from Pete, and ended up renting the top two floors to tenants while our family lived on the bottom floor from the time I was in fourth grade through eighth grade.

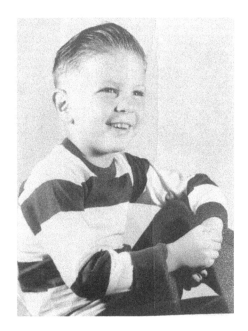

Me at age four or five

Our family lived above every business we ever had and all the years we were growing up, David and I shared a room – as well as other childhood milestones like the measles and the mumps. During the time that our family lived over a bar in Paterson, the layout of the apartment was such that David and I had to go outside of the building and upstairs to use the bathroom; a back room in the bar had secret cubby holes from Prohibition days that we loved to explore. I remember David and I sharing a laugh the first time we walked into our shared room in that apartment because the room's one window was positioned right up against a brick wall, so not only did we have no view, but we had absolutely no natural light coming in either. At the place we eventually lived in above our store in Bergenfield, David used to enjoy laying in that apartment's bay window and staring up at the stars, maybe dreaming of all of the places life would take him when he was old enough to move out and make his own choices.

*Me (age eight) and my younger brother David during my
holy communion at St. John's Catholic Church in Paterson, NJ*

I started peddling produce door to door with my dad from the age of five, with Pop driving a truck up and down the streets of local towns and me knocking on doors on one side of the street and David, once he was old enough, covering doors on the other side. Pop filled the truck with seasonal items – tomatoes, peaches, and watermelon in the summer, apples in the fall, etc. – and us kids would knock on a door, say "hey, lady, want to buy a tomato?" or whatever we were offering, and they'd come out to the truck to make their purchase. My dad always knew what sold well to people of different ethnicities or the ingredients they liked to cook with at that time and, for example, made sure to load up the truck with fruit when we went into certain neighborhoods and more kale and vegetables when we visited others.

An old photo of me (right) and my younger brother David selling watermelons –
"two for $1.25" – off the back of Pop's truck in the early 1950s

One of the items David and I helped our dad peddle door-to-door was bananas, a fruit which became associated with a life-long fear of mine. Back then, we'd go down to the New York piers with Pop and get the bananas as they were coming off the ship. They were sold in stalks, maybe 9 or 10 hands to a stalk, and my father would buy around 50 stalks, bring them back to our house, and hang them in the basement to ripen because they often came off of the ship on the green side. Because they were shipped at a cool temperature, spiders and snakes that were sometimes hidden in the stalks would go dormant but wake up once they felt the heat of the house – an experience which could be frightening for us kids. For years mom would never let me or my brother go in the basement and to this day I'm absolutely petrified of snakes. These days, things are different and bananas are cut, bagged, and boxed right in the field and shipped to the U.S. – thankfully no surprises (and none in my wife Bette's delicious banana bread recipe, either)!

Bette's Best Banana Bread

(no spiders or snakes, I promise!)

2 ripe bananas, mashed

1/2 cup butter, melted

1 cup sugar

2 eggs

1 teaspoon vanilla

1 teaspoon baking powder

1 teaspoon baking soda

Pinch of salt

½ cup sour cream

1¾ cups all-purpose flour

Walnuts (optional)

Preheat oven to 350 degrees. In a large mixing bowl, mix butter into the mashed bananas, then fold in the sugar, eggs, sour cream, and vanilla. Sprinkle the baking soda, baking powder, and salt over the mixture and stir together. Add the flour last and stir until well-blended (mixing in any walnuts if desired). Pour mixture into a buttered 4x8-inch loaf pan and bake for 50 minutes. Cool on a rack. Remove from pan and slice to serve.

In addition to going door-to-door, we used to peddle produce at various markets around the area too. One of them was Frankie's Market, an open-air farmer's market on Route 17 in Lodi, NJ that was open from Friday through Sunday night (and where a Pathmark would reside decades later). When I was little, maybe six or seven, my father and his brothers had a stand there and we used to go there on Friday nights, come home on Sunday night, and sleep in the truck in between. I helped out by taking in customers' single dollars from my perch on a bushel basket of string beans and giving them back change (an image of which my nephew Kurt captured in an original rendering at the very beginning of this book). The problem was, what do you do with all of the cash you collect to avoid being robbed? Back then, string beans came in high-hat bushels three feet high; we'd take all of the dollars, stash them in the bushels of beans like they were produce, and then put the bushels back in the truck with the tops on them so that they didn't attract attention. On Monday morning, we'd go back to the family home on Humphrey Street in Englewood, where Pop and his brothers would dump the bushels out, collect all the cash, and split it between them.

We always had food on the table during those years, though not much of anything else. We had very little meat and ate what was on the truck, which was mostly vegetables, but my mom was the best 'Italian' cook of all her Italian sisters-in-law and made something wonderful out of everything. I especially remember the potatoes and string beans she made in a tomato-type sauce as well as her stuffed peppers with black olives and her great burgundy-colored sauces, to which she'd add meatballs and raisins or an item that didn't sell that day.

It was amazing what my mom could do on little or no money to make every meal and holiday special for us. At Halloween, rather than carving out a pumpkin and wasting its contents, my mother used to decorate our pumpkins intact so that she could use their interior pulp and seeds in her cooking after the holiday was over. She'd use a carrot or parsnip to make a long, witchy nose, red peppers for lips, radishes for eyes, and string beans for eyebrows, then slice potatoes to make ears and craft "hair" out of fennel tops. At Christmas, I'll never forget her wrapping navel oranges in colored foil or paper and putting them in my and David's stockings, a tradition we looked forward to every year; we were always excited to unwrap them because citrus was a novelty shipped in from Florida and California and not native to New Jersey. Mom never threw away or wasted anything – even the peels from those oranges, which she'd put in a used tin pie plate with water and place on the radiator to give our house a great citrusy aroma. I still wrap oranges in foil and Christmas paper every year on my show as a tribute to my mother.

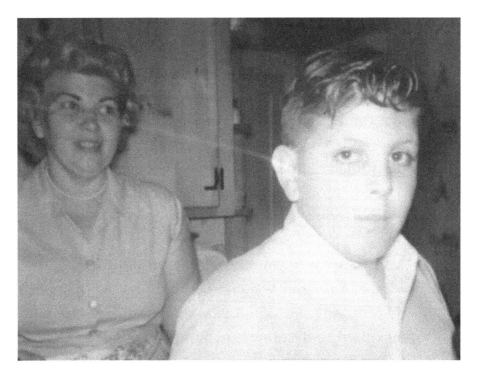

Me and my beloved Mom in the 1950s

When it came to feeding the family affordably in our post-WWII New Jersey kitchen, stews and one-pot dishes were a go-to. One of my father's favorite dishes ever since he'd been a kid was *gumbroit*, a ratatouille-like concoction made with eggplant, squash, tomatoes, and other vegetables – especially the way his mother Maria (whom we called Nonna) made it. Whenever my mother made gumbroit, Pop would say, "that's good, but not as good as my mother's," which drove Mom crazy because she learned to cook from my father's mother and made it just the way Nonna had taught her….or so she thought.

My nonna, Maria Napolitano

For a long time, Mom tried to figure out what she could be doing wrong, until it finally dawned on her that Nonna used vegetables that were spotted, bruised, and beyond ripe – stuff other customers wouldn't buy. So Mom went right down to the store, picked out all the spotted eggplants, squash, and tomatoes, and took them home to make gumbroit, Nonna-style. It was a hit and my father absolutely loved it!

Nonna Napolitano's Gumbroit

(don't hesitate to used bruised and/or overripe ingredients for great flavor – Nonna's secret!)

3 tablespoons olive oil

2 onions, diced

2 cloves fresh garlic

2 zucchinis, cubed

1 eggplant, cubed

2 peppers, diced

1 pound fresh string beans, cut into pieces

2 fresh tomatoes

1 tablespoon oregano

Dash of salt

In a large skillet, pour in the oil, add the diced onions and garlic, and sauté until golden brown. Add the zucchini, eggplant, peppers, and string beans and sauté until fork tender. Add the fresh tomatoes, oregano, and salt. Stir and sauté for an additional 5 minutes and serve!

As peddlers, peaches were a big hit for us and provided endless imagery for me during my childhood. Peaches are actually very fuzzy – a measure taken by Mother Nature to protect them from the sun – but most people have no idea how much fuzz peaches actually have because by the time they reach the market, 90% of it has been removed by machines. Francis Johnson, one of the farmers we dealt with, grew peaches on his farm in Ramsey, NJ and the big red barn that served as his packing site was so laden with peach fuzz clinging to the rafters that it always looked like a white castle to me as a kid.

Tomatoes were also a huge seller for us when we peddled them door-to-door and they still bring back vivid memories for me. Pre-1959, we used to go down to the dock and pick up hundreds of 3-4-pound wooden boxes of tomatoes imported from Cuba; I'd then tag along with Pop as we'd go to every bar from Jersey City, NJ to Nyack, NY and sell them. Bar owners and their customers loved them because they were vine-ripened coming all the way from Cuba and tasted just like Jersey tomatoes. That's how we started in the tomato business.

I remember as a kid out on the truck with Pop, he'd stop at some little store at lunchtime to buy a loaf of Italian bread and then we'd find a place where we could pull off to the side of the road. He'd put down a piece of cardboard for a cutting board, slice the bread, cut up a tomato and an onion, and make tomato sandwiches for us. With the perfect ripe red tomato and good bread, there's nothing better and I've never been able to duplicate that incredible taste ever since. To this day, even though I can afford them, I'd rather have a good tomato sandwich like Pop made it or a plate of escarole and beans like my mom prepared it than a steak or lobster.

Pop's Tomato Sandwich

(the great taste of simpler times)

2 slices Italian semolina bread

1 medium-to-large ripe Jersey tomato, sliced

2-3 thin slices sweet onion

Olive oil

Balsamic vinegar

Dried oregano

Salt and freshly ground black pepper to taste

Hot peppers (optional)

For this sandwich, you need the best semolina bread, perfectly ripe tomatoes, and the best olive oil. We always had olive oil and vinegar in the truck, but if we were near a delicatessen or general store, sometimes my father would buy a little jar of mayonnaise and use that too. If you're using mayonnaise, spread a thin layer on both slices of bread, cover one piece with a thick layer of tomato slices, then the thinly-sliced onions. Sprinkle some hot peppers on top. Dress with olive oil, vinegar, oregano, salt, and pepper to taste. Top with the second slice of bread. One bite and you'll know it's summer.

*Carrying on the legacy: Enjoying a Jersey tomato
sandwich with my nephew Kurt on a hot summer day*

In 1956-1957, around the time I was in fifth or sixth grade and
we lived in Tenafly, my parents capitalized on some retail opportunities there and in nearby Bergenfield which proved to be a
turning point for our family in many ways.

There was a Sinclair gas station with a big green dinosaur logo
on its sign on the corner of Washington Avenue and Liberty
Road in Bergenfield, across from the Teaneck Armory, and one
day my mother pulled in for gas and noticed an empty lot next

door. She asked the gas station owner if he could rent her the space so that she could park in the lot and sell something off of our truck. She then asked my dad to buy her a load of watermelons to sell. He went to the Washington Market by the Hudson River, bought her 150-200 watermelons, and she put up a sign. He drove by during the day to see her sitting there, and by the end of the day, to his surprise, she'd sold the entire load!

Being the good husband that he was, he bought her *two* loads of watermelons the next day – and she sold them both! Soon after, he stopped driving the bus for Red & Tan and joined her on that corner. Eventually, my dad rented space for them on a site catty-corner from the gas station alongside Pelka's Rainbow Diner on Washington Avenue and every day he and my mother would buy produce, lay it out on rugs, and sell it. It eventually became a successful roadside stand that we operated from around Easter through Thanksgiving – a business my mother had in fact started!

Down the street on Washington Avenue in Bergenfield, next to what would later be Libonati's Tavern, there was a burnt-out restaurant, formerly Dotter's Diner, sitting on a piece of property that the owner was asking $18,000 or $20,000 for. It might as well have been a million dollars to my father, but he had a vision. He borrowed the money from family members, bought the property, and had a company demolish the diner and bury it in the ground, which was the cheapest way to get rid of it at the time. He erected a tent on the property to house our roadside stand, but it was difficult to manage in inclement weather, so Pop had another idea.

In the late 1950s, as was the case in so many suburban communities in post-WWII America, a local company called Alfis Brothers was advertising their ability to put up spec Cape Cod-style homes for $9,999. One day in 1958-1959 Pop knocked on their office doors and asked them to put up a building for him on an "I promise I'll pay you" basis. While an honor-system pledge like that would obviously never be good enough collateral today, they saw that he was a hard-working immigrant and agreed to build him the building, and he did eventually pay them back every cent. Per his request, they put up a two-story building on our property, with the bottom half housing two garage-type spaces and the top floor containing an apartment with three small bedrooms, a kitchen, a living room, and a bathroom for our family.

My sister Louise Anne (LuAnne) was born on January 3rd, 1959 and later that year, our family moved from Tenafly to Bergenfield and officially opened our brick-and-mortar store, Napolitano's Produce. It represented our family's version of the "American Dream" and would operate for nearly a half-century.

Me and my sister LuAnne (all grown up!) at a recent family party

Ironically, the ground in which Pop buried the old diner – and upon which he built our new building – continued to sink as the wood and building materials in the old structure rotted and he ended up having to fill in the paving in our store's parking lot every year to repair the sinkhole that was created. I think that the $500 he paid up front to have the diner buried ended up costing our family $20,000 for the repaving we had to undertake every year for the next three decades to fix it – a family joke which always gave us a laugh! In this case, the old adage that "you get what you pay for" was never truer!

The original Dotter's Diner in Bergenfield, NJ, which became a burnt-out, vacant restaurant. My father ultimately demolished it in order to build Napolitano's Produce on its site in 1959.

CHAPTER 2

'SUCCESS IN STORE'

When we peddled produce door-to-door or sold items at our roadside stand, we sold what we wanted to sell and what was seasonal and in demand. In our new store, however, we had to carry items that didn't always sell well but which made for a "complete" store so that customers would have a one-stop-shop experience and come back.

Our store was open from 8 a.m. to 7 p.m. on Mondays through Saturdays and from 8 a.m. to 2 p.m. on Sundays. Discipline was important to Pop and he always impressed upon us that to be successful, you couldn't burn the candle at both ends; as a result, I never needed an alarm clock because my body came to know our daily routine on its own. Before school on weekdays, David and I would get up at around 6 a.m. and go outside to our refrigerator, which sat in an old milk truck parked under a tree. Items like lettuce, berries, grapes, and other perishable items had to be taken out of the fridge and brought into the store so that Mom could set them up. Pop was already at the Washington Market buying produce since 12-1 a.m. and usually got back by around 7:30 each morning to help open the store. After school at around 3 p.m., David and I went back to work, taking care of customers and unloading trucks until about 6 p.m., when we'd help break down the store and put items back in the fridge. I started driving the truck when I was 13. Though my mother always warned my dad "don't let Pete drive!", we wouldn't even be to the corner before he was trading seats with me so that he could sleep while I drove to the Washington Street market along the Hudson River in New York City on Sunday nights.

A rendering of our family store in Bergenfield, NJ in the 1990s by my nephew, Kurt; built in 1959, the two-story structure housed our business downstairs and our family upstairs

Our store opened the week before Easter every March or April and closed for the season on Christmas Eve. In addition to selling produce during the season, we also sold holiday items like pumpkins at Halloween, Christmas trees, and Easter plants to make money. During the store's hiatus from January-March when we had nothing to sell, and even before we had the store, Pop did odd jobs like bartending while we kids picked up neighborhood jobs and delivered phone books to help make ends meet. Back in the day, homeowners were supposed to sign for a phone book when deliveries were made, but Pop figured out a way to sign for them himself to save time. It wasn't so honest, but he made the process more efficient and the phone book company eventually gave him the better territories because he delivered so many!

We worked every day and all weekend long and once school ended, we would work full-time all summer with no vacation, which I hated; David and I were probably the only kids who never looked forward to the summer because for us it meant full work days. While David ended up getting a Master's degree in finance and becoming extremely successful in the finance industry, he's always resented the way we were brought up, feeling that our parents robbed us of our childhood. I don't think of it that way – I just think that we were poor and that was the mentality. It's just what it was. As early as five years old, I knew I'd either be a bank robber or go to work. When you're poor, things can go either way, but it's about the choices you make and I always knew I'd end up going to work.

When it came to running the business, living right over the store made for a much easier commute to work for all of us than when we lived in Tenafly and ran the stand in Bergenfield. Bergenfield was a very blue-collar town with pockets of Italian, Jewish, and German families who worked hard and cooked at home, and business was very good from the beginning. People bought food close to the time that they were going to consume it and customers (mostly women/mothers) shopped at our store once and even twice a day. Though I suspect that our prices could probably have been a little higher, our family started to make a living and as we got busier, we started hiring relatives to help out at the store, including my uncles Frank, Freddy, and Ritzie and my Aunt Lena and her kids.

Our store in the 1960s

In the back of our store, we had a stove that my mom used to cook meals for all of us and our help during the day. Her sizzling pans of escarole and beans or potatoes and string beans would smell so good throughout the store that customers would ask for my mom's recipes and then buy the ingredients. Mom was a true original and was definitely ahead of her time when it came to utilizing the power of cooking demos to tantalize shoppers and sell products!

Her delicious cooking won me over as well and escarole and beans remains one of my favorite dishes even now. When we were kids, Mom used to let me and David choose whatever we wanted for our birthday dinners. I remember that David would choose steak or leg of lamb, but no matter what, I always chose escarole and beans – leading Mom to joke that she loved to feed me because I was the cheap date in the family! To this day, even though I can afford fancier and far more expensive fare, I'd rather have a plate of escarole and beans just like my mom used to prepare it.

Mom's Escarole and Beans

(Makes 6 servings)

2 heads escarole

¼ cup olive oil

5 cloves garlic, chopped

2 19-ounce cans cannellini beans, drained

1 teaspoon salt

1 teaspoon freshly ground black pepper

1 teaspoon hot crushed red pepper flakes

Cut off one inch from the bottoms of the escarole leaves and discard. Break off the escarole leaves and rinse well. Fill a saucepan about one-third with water, place the escarole leaves in the pan, cover, and steam until tender (or place in a steamer tray designed to fit over a pot or saucepan). Drain in a colander and set aside. Heat the oil in the saucepan and sauté the garlic until well-browned. Add the escarole and remaining ingredients and stir. Cover and simmer for 5 minutes, then serve and enjoy!

All through 1960 and 1961, our store kept getting busier and summertime was definitely our busiest season. We sourced product from the Washington Market in downtown Manhattan (which ultimately evolved into the Hunts Point Market in The Bronx in 1968), the Newark Farmers market, which took place every Sunday night, and local farms throughout New Jersey and southern New York. Tomatoes were among our most popular items – we'd sell 700 peach basket-loads a week at the store! – as well as other items like corn and peaches from great local providers in north Jersey like Demarest Farms in Hillsdale, DiPiero's Farm and Tice's Farm in Woodcliff Lake, and Trautwein's Farm in Closter as well as Smith Farms in New City, NY. Pop had a 24-foot truck that he'd load up with local produce from front to back and we'd sell out every day. Needless to say, we got very friendly with all of the local farmers in our area as well as a number of farms we did business with in southern New Jersey.

Work was what we knew and our family missed a lot of holidays because we worked through them. On Thanksgiving, we'd open the store early for customers, work until 2 p.m., and then head upstairs to eat the Thanksgiving meal Mom prepared for us. Afterwards, Pop would take a quick nap, change his clothes, get into his truck, and head upstate to New York, New England, or Canada to bring back a load of Christmas trees that we could sell at our store. I just thought that this was what everyone's father did. We sold thousands of trees, all under $1.99, standing out in the cold by a fire barrel. We'd end up putting up our own Christmas tree at midnight on Christmas Eve. Once again, for years when I was younger, I just thought that's what everybody did.

My mother and the son of a family friend working in our store around 1962

CHAPTER 3

LIFE WITH POP

To run the store on a daily basis, we ate in shifts and, believe it or not, my parents even attended funerals in shifts because Pop wouldn't close the store for any reason. Given the perishable field we were in, Pop never wanted to give other stores an opportunity to take over our business. Over the years, competitors sprang up in town and tried to open similar produce operations, but Pop would give a customer produce for free before he'd lose a customer to another store. He understood that customers might want to try something new or patronize another business located somewhere else as a novelty, but he believed that they'd always come back if we took good care of them, so we were very focused on servicing our customers in any way and at all hours.

I remember one time when I was in my late teens/early 20s and had just proudly bought a '65 Chevy convertible for $3,300. Our family was having Thanksgiving dinner when the Clinton

Inn in Tenafly called to say that they needed more lettuce. Our trucks were all locked up for the holiday at that point, so my father made me deliver six cases of lettuce to them in my new car with the top down. His obsession with servicing customers at all costs may not have been the healthiest or most balanced approach to doing business, especially for me and our family, but that was his work ethic and mentality and we understood what it was and accepted it.

Not everyone else did, however. I'll never forget when I was around 16 and a student at Bergenfield High School, our football coach stopped me in the hallway one day and asked me if I'd be interested in trying out for the football team. I was a big kid in school and, even though Pop couldn't understand the point of a bunch of guys throwing a ball around and getting piled on and shoved to the ground once they caught it, I'd always loved football. I told the coach that I'd love to try out but that I had to work every day after school in my father's store, at which point he said that he'd call my father and tell him that I had my whole life to work. "Oh boy, here we go," I thought. I already knew what Pop's answer would be, but I told the coach to knock himself out anyway and gave him the store phone number. Sure enough, a couple of days later the coach informed me that he'd called Pop and that, after asking him about the possibility of my playing football for the school, Pop asked the coach how much he was going to pay me. And that was the beginning and end of my football career!

That was Pop for you, born in a different country with a different set of rules. It was often hard to reconcile, especially around friends of mine whose fathers were professionals; they lived in nice houses with dads who were doctors and lawyers while I was living next to a cemetery with a father who would pick me up in an old truck with bananas hanging off of it. Growing up, I was often embarrassed to talk about my father and share what he did for a living, especially when I was younger and Pop was a peddler. As a fourth grader at the Smith School in Tenafly, I remember being asked to write a paper about my life and what I hoped to be when I grew up. In this document, dutifully typed by my mother (and which I still have today!), I shared my aspiration to be a lawyer someday – there was no mention of a life in the produce business, that's for sure! (Ironically, while a career in the legal field didn't prove to be in the cards for me, I ended up running into my fourth grade teach, Mrs. Urban, at a golf course 40 years later and she confirmed that she remembered that paper I'd written and thought it had been great!).

Living and working with my father day in and day out at the store, we bickered a lot and my relationship with him was very strained. Though I eventually grew to understand that certain life experiences he'd endured – including the poverty he was born into, the wartime carnage he witnessed, and the stress of raising a family and running a successful business in America – played a great hand in shaping who he was, Pop could be verbally abusive. He never hit or got physical with Mom or any of us kids, but he'd often yell at me in the store, call me stupid or tell me that I'd never amount to anything, or purposely knock something over and then tell me to pick it up. I remember my Aunt Lena (Pop's sister) screaming at him to stop yelling at us the way he did. Though he'd occasionally apologize, it drove me crazy and I often looked at him like he had two heads or wanted to strangle him. Later in life, however, I came to accept that I hadn't walked in his shoes – he'd done the best he could and passed on what he knew, good and bad. He came from a volatile family of 17 brothers and three sisters (all of whom ended up living within five miles of each other) who fought like cats and dogs and could then be hugging each other, though all I ever seem to remember was them fighting.

Pop was a good provider, but he had no education and was always looking for the next opportunity; he was never satisfied. He was also a womanizer, which Mom was well aware of. I'm sure it upset her, but she never expressed that to us kids. While what Pop did wasn't right, I think that back then those were just the times we lived in. You just settled for what things were and tried to see the good in what you had; there was food on the table and the business and family were intact. Pop never hit my mom, but to my mind he did something worse – he humiliated her by running around with other women.

He could be self-centered and cruel in other ways too. I'll never forget the time my mom made me a chocolate cake for my ninth or tenth birthday. As she got ready to go to work to help support our family, she left the cake on the kitchen table with a note to my father saying "this is Peter's birthday cake – please don't eat it!" because she knew him all too well. Sure enough, when Pop returned home, he and his friends ate the whole cake. Though my family laughs about it now, the incident reflects Pop's sometimes selfish nature and still touches a raw nerve for me nearly 70 years later.

My father's own sisters used to tell my mom that she should leave him, but she loved him and, despite his wandering eye, he was otherwise good to her. Despite how poor we were, I remember that Pop never argued with Mom when she gave our hard-earned money to members of her family to help them financially.

In stark contrast to Pop's more stoic and volatile demeanor, Mom was incredibly loyal and nurturing and, in her eyes, her kids could do no wrong. My mom's father had been an alcoholic and her mother was a nurse who'd kept their family together financially, so mom knew a thing or two about being a strong partner. At one point, my dad bought a bar in Paterson and she'd bartend there during the day and he'd take over at night; when we opened Napolitano's Produce, she was the true force behind its success. Mom was a great cook, extremely hard-working, and always made us laugh; she was a wonderful person and mother and she and I were very close.

While there were tough times, there were laughs and good times in our household too, especially when our large and colorful cast of extended family members got together. I remember taking family trips down to the Jersey shore and once to Niagara Falls. On Sunday afternoons in the summer, we'd close the store and go to Crestwood Lake in Allendale, NJ to swim and eat with our aunts, uncles, and cousins, and to this day our family still organizes a cousins' party every year.

Mostly, however, we worked. Just before I attended my 50th high school reunion in 2013, New Jersey's *Bergen Record* newspaper published an article about me and my life; at the reunion, I can't tell you how many of my former classmates came up to me to say that they'd read the piece and had no idea that I'd balanced school and homework with such a rigorous and near full-time work schedule at the store.

*Manging en mass! Eating and catching up at a
Napolitano family event in the 1950s*

CHAPTER 4

TAKING THE NEXT STEP

In 1962, when I was around 16, a few friends and I decided to go to a bowling alley in Bergenfield near our store and Pelka's Rainbow Diner to meet some girls from a nearby town. There were three or four girls there when we walked in and I remember hearing the song *Duke of Earl* by Gene Chandler playing on the jukebox. One of the girls really stood out to me and, as strange as this seems — because at that age, who knows about marriage or even love? — I turned to my friend Dennis and told him that I was going to marry that girl someday. I ultimately did – we got married five years later and celebrated our 55th anniversary in 2022!

That girl's name was Elizabeth (Bette) Lynn Donaldson from Tenafly and she was 14 or 15 at the time; I was two grades ahead of her. I was very shy around girls as a teen and my friend Richie actually went out with her first, but whenever I could, I'd get a ride from someone or hitchhike to see Bette so that we could hang out. We talked a lot as friends but I really liked her from the start. I think that there's one person in the world for you if you're lucky enough to find them and she was my person; we started dating and made a real connection.

Though I was a jealous boyfriend and was always afraid that she'd leave me for someone else, she calmed those fears because she was such a good and honest girl in addition to being beautiful, funny, easy to talk to, and mixing well with my friends. Plus, she and I were friends, which I think is the most important thing for a successful relationship. Bette and I have had plenty of arguments over the years, but she's still my best friend, and she showed early on that she had what it takes to be a supportive partner too; after I got my driver's license at age 17, I'd sometimes sell Christmas trees or Easter plants in a lot on my own for extra money and Bette would be right there alongside me helping me sell them.

Me and Bette, ages 16 and 14

Bette was the youngest of five kids and had two older brothers and two older sisters. Her mother, Julie, was Italian, and her father, Charles (whom everyone called "Bucky"), was of Italian and Scottish descent. Bucky was a very nice but very tough guy and, like most of the working-class people in our area at that time, he held down two or three jobs; among his different occupations, he'd been a professional boxer, then owned a luncheonette in Bergenfield and drove a cab. Bette's family of seven lived on the second floor of her grandmother's house and always had food on the table but not a lot of extras. However, their house was on a full acre of property and they had ducks, chickens, gardens, and fig, peach, and other fruit trees in the backyard.

At that age I thought I knew everything, but Bette's family was very resourceful and I learned a lot from them. I remember her grandfather Nino digging a trench along a slope in their backyard using just a shovel and then lining it with clay pots so that he could bring water from the house out to the back to water the garden. And I'll never forget the time Nino asked me to help him cover their 15-foot-high fig tree one fall to prepare it for winter. I watched in amazement as he directed me to help him lasso the tree, bend it nearly in half, and stake and wrap it with towels and anything else he had because I thought for sure that we'd killed that tree. I was even more positive of that the following spring when we unwrapped it, cut the strings, and it remained depressingly bent over, but Bette kept telling me, "just wait!" Sure enough, a week later it was standing fully upright and later that fall it yielded the biggest and most beautiful figs you've ever seen. There's been a special place in my heart for figs ever since!

Bette's family members were working-class people like us, but they didn't work the way we did. They sat at the table and ate meals together like a family, went on family vacations, and attended weddings, funerals, and other events as a family, not in shifts like we Napolitanos did to ensure that someone was always there to cover the business. In other words, they didn't prioritize work ahead of important family rituals and quality time and I found myself gravitating to their "enlightened" definition of family.

Bucky was a tough guy, even in his seventies, but he and Julie were wonderful people and became like parents to me. Years later when I took over the store with no money and was too proud to ask for help, Julie would secretly take me aside and give me money but make me promise not to tell Bucky; Bucky would secretly do the same and make me promise not to tell Julie. Julie was also the first to step in and watch our kids so that Bette and I could work. They were always there for me and were the first people I'd repay whenever money flowed in.

Bette's parents, Julie and Charles "Bucky" Donaldson, in the early 1980s. They were always there for me!

While Bette's parents liked me, we got along great, and they knew that I was a hard-working guy, the same wasn't initially true of one of her older siblings. Her second-oldest brother was a very smart guy with a doctorate and was concerned that I only had a high school education; he feared that I had no future and shared that opinion with Bette in a letter he wrote to her before we got married. Though Bette was offended by his candor, I wasn't; I understood his concern for his sister. I and my family used to peddle produce on Columbus Drive where she lived and her family knew mine; some members of my extended family were thugs, gangsters, and otherwise colorful characters who had a bad reputation, but I always used to say, "that's my family, that's not me."

That's not to say that I was any kind of saint; I definitely got into my share of teenage shenanigans. One night when I was 17, I went out drinking with a bunch of friends and ended up getting a tattoo of Bette's initials (B.D.) on my arm. I remember Pop coming in early the next morning from the market to find me dazed and hung over in the kitchen.

He eyed my new artwork and sized up the situation quickly. "Hey sailor, time to get to work!" he said.

"I don't feel so good, Pop," I complained.

"If you think *this* is bad," he joked, "it'll be even worse when you get there."

Another time when I was 18, I went to a bar in New York with a group of my friends and we ended up getting arrested for fighting. All of my friends immediately called their parents to get bailed out, but I held back, which led the cop to come over and ask me if I wanted to contact my parents. "Not on your life!" I snapped. "I'd rather sit in jail than tell my dad!" I was afraid of disappointing him.

Make no mistake, we had fun in those days too. One of Bette's lifelong friends was a wonderful gal named Adele, whose father, Alfred Garbarino (affectionately known as "Gabby") had a great restaurant in Tenafly named "Gabby's." He also had a summer house in Lavallette, NJ and would always open the house to Adele and her sister's friends and boyfriends and cook for us. Among our gang's favorite items was a delicious southern Italian dish he made with Swiss chard called malfatti, which was similar to meat-filled dumplings. All these years later, Gabby is still in my heart and the taste of malfatti always brings back wonderful memories of a man who treated all of us kids like family when we were growing up in the 1960s. He made a big impression on me, just like malfatti will make on you!

Gabby's Malfatti

(Makes 4 to 6 servings)

½ cup (1 stick) butter

1 cup onions, finely chopped

4 cups Swiss chard, cooked, drained, and chopped

2 pounds ground beef

1¼ cups grated Parmesan cheese

4 eggs

¾ cup bread crumbs

½ cup flour

4 cups tomato sauce

Preheat oven to 350 degrees. In a skillet, melt the butter, add the onion, and sauté until lightly browned. In a large bowl, mix the sautéed onion, Swiss chard, ground beef, 1 cup grated cheese, eggs, and bread crumbs. Take a small handful of the mixture and form into sausage-like rolls about 3 inches long. Place some flour in a dish and roll each malfatti in flour until well-coated. Bring a large saucepan half full of water to a boil, place the malfatti rolls into the pan, and boil them until they float to the top, about 5-7 minutes. Remove them with a slotted spoon and drain. Cover the bottom of the baking pan with tomato sauce and place the malfatti in the pan in a single layer. Cover with sauce and sprinkle with the remaining Parmesan cheese, bake for approximately 20-30 minutes, and enjoy!

*Let the good times roll! Hanging out at Gabby's
beach house in Lavallette, NJ in the early 1960s*

I graduated from Bergenfield High School in 1963 and Pop, who placed a high value on education, perhaps because he hadn't been given the opportunity himself, thought I needed to go to college. I'd been a decent student in high school and had always passed my classes, but I knew that I was a working guy who wasn't necessarily made for university life. To please him, however, I went to an interview for a college in Emporia, KS that was advertising for students in our area and got accepted. I remember being a wreck when Bette came with me to the airport to see me off. I didn't want to leave her and was practically crying; I even shared those sentiments in a desperate, hostage-like note that I scribbled to her in the back seat of my parents' car on the way to the airport – I wanted to jump out of the car or somehow miss the plane!

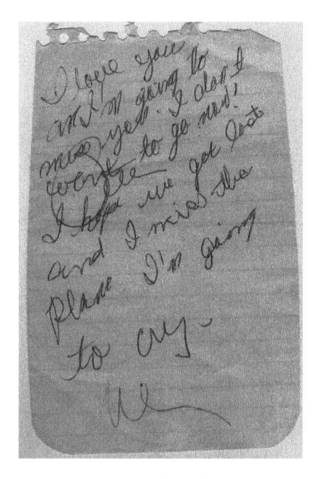

The actual note I scrawled to Bette in the car as I reluctantly left for college in 1963....she kept it all of these years!

I eventually arrived at the College of Emporia, where the terrain was so flat that you could practically see New Jersey from Kansas. I was assigned to a dorm room the size of a closet with five other guys and as the days went by, students were dropping out left and right; though the school started out with thousands of freshmen, the experience proved to be so unpleasant that they ended up with only a few hundred upperclassmen. Within three days, I also packed it in and came home. Pop refused to send me money for plane fare; when I told him that I didn't care and would hitchhike home, he finally relented and sent me money, but he didn't pick me up at the airport. Instead, he sent his friend, Wordy Talino, to pick me up. I ended up staying with Wordy for a month because Pop wouldn't allow me to come home, until my mother finally intervened and cleared the way.

Pop didn't talk to me for that month and I felt like a failure, but the school definitely wasn't a good fit for me. However, so as not to disappoint my dad, I tried my hand at college again, this time at Windham College in Putney, VT, a town which, until recently, was home to the largest basket store in the world. It was a decent school and I established a routine where I would park my car in Brattleboro (since we couldn't park on campus as freshmen) and drive down to New Jersey to see Bette on weekends. That November, I remember seeing other students crying on campus and learned that JFK had just been shot. By December, I knew that I was done. Though my brother David successfully pursued higher education and I made sure that both of my own kids went to college, I decided that college wasn't for me and I came home for good.

Pop was mad at me again for dropping out and treated me like I was a bum, so I got a job as an apprentice plumber for a year and then ended up working for another plumber in Tenafly. Right around that time – in the mid-1960s – I was drafted into the Army and proceeded to go to the Induction Center at 1 Whitehall Street in New York City for a physical. Years earlier, when I was about six or seven, I'd had a mysterious illness (possibly classified as rheumatic fever at the time) that had kept me in bed for most of the second grade and required me to take a dose of penicillin every day; this may have contributed to what the Army physician claimed was a heart murmur. Two weeks later, I received a letter classifying me as a "1Y" (serving only in a time of national emergency), a development that kept me out of Vietnam.

Bette and I had talked about getting engaged before, but she'd been holding off until my future appeared more certain. Late in the summer of 1966, when Bette and her family took a three-week trip out to California to visit her older brother Charles ("Donnie"), who was a Marine, and his wife and kids, I missed her terribly and knew the time was right. I asked Bette's friend Linda to help me find her an engagement ring and ended up giving the jeweler in Englewood a $1,000 deposit – everything I had in life at that point – and a commitment to repay the rest. The jeweler knew my family and that's the only reason he trusted me for the rest of the money.

When Bette and her family returned from California, I picked them all up at the airport. I nervously took her father aside and declared that "I want to marry your daughter," to which he replied "talk to Julie" and smiled. When we got back to their house in Tenafly, I anxiously approached Julie, but she already suspected what I was up to.

"You want to marry Bette?" Julie asked me.

"More than anything in the world," I said, "and I'll always take care of her." She saw how sincere I was and agreed to let me propose to Bette.

I stashed the ring in the glove compartment of my new Chevy convertible and the next time Bette and I went out, I asked her to get something out of the glove compartment for me. She saw the box and immediately said "Oh my God!" I was so nervous and all I could think to say was, "so, is it a yes or no?" Happily, she said yes!

Bette and I on our wedding day in June 1967. We had to change the day of our wedding from a Saturday to a Sunday because Pop refused to close the store on a Saturday to attend the event

Bette and I got engaged on September 27th, 1966, when I was 21 and she was 18, and her parents threw us a nice engagement party. We began planning our wedding and selected a particular Saturday the following August at a banquet hall called The Fiesta on Route 17 in Wood-Ridge, NJ for the reception. When I told Pop about our plan, he just looked at me and said "have a good time," because it was a Saturday and he never closed the store on that day. I wanted to strangle him, but I went back to Bette and told her that we had to find another date to ensure his attendance. We ended up getting married earlier, on June 11th, 1967 – a Sunday – and went to Puerto Rico and the Virgin Islands on our honeymoon. During our last day in Puerto Rico, halfway through our trip, we got a call that Bette's grandfather had died and we rushed home to pay our last respects to a man she'd grown up with and loved.

Once I was a married man, I decided that I needed to make our family business my career. I expressed that wish to Pop and was committed to making it work so that I could give Bette a good life. About 10 years earlier, Mom and Pop had started going to Florida during our store's hiatus every January-February (usually staying in a motel in Miami Beach), and they'd recently put down deeper roots in the Sunshine State by buying a house in Boca Raton; at that point, I knew that my dad would only work at the store for a couple more years. Since graduating from high school, I'd butted heads with my father quite a bit and had quit working at the store more than a few times to pursue other jobs – in addition to plumbing, I'd also sold Britannica encyclopedias and worked for a collection agency – but I'd always come back. And now, despite often being at odds with him, I once again came back to work for my father.

With my full-time job at the store and Bette's job – she'd always been good at typing and stenography and landed a secretarial position right out of high school – she and I started our life together. We rented a one-bedroom apartment at the Steuben Arms complex in River Edge, NJ for $150 per month, ultimately upgrading to an apartment with a dishwasher for $155 (to which my father said, "you had to spend the extra $5?").

Disco days! Me and Bette in the early-mid 1970s

I was working seven days a week and Bette was working five. Bette soon got pregnant but had a miscarriage, which devastated her. Our dog at the store, Lassie, had puppies, and I brought one home for Bette, who was a devoted animal lover, to help cheer her up. She named the puppy Chips and loved and spoiled that dog beyond belief; Chips became her baby. Beginning with Chips, our house was always full of animals.

As it turned out, four or five months later, Bette got pregnant again and our son Peter was born in February 1969. At the end of that year, Pop informed me that he was getting out of the business and said that I could buy the store from him or go find a job. Pop ended up selling the building out from under me to the Libonatis, owners of the tavern next door, for $70,000 because he knew I had no money. Though they didn't necessarily want it, they bought it because we shared common property and felt that owning it would protect both of our properties and investments. Once Pop sold the property, I secured a lease for our space from the Libonatis and they were kind enough to rent it to me for a very reasonable amount. After I secured the lease, Pop came to me asking me to sign a $10,000 note for the trucks and equipment in the store. It took me three years to repay it but paying off that debt was the most important thing in my life because it removed that obligation from my back, physically and emotionally. While I wasn't necessarily resentful about the arrangement, I definitely think Pop could have made things easier for me.

I was scared as hell to take over the store at age 24 with little or no money and a new wife and infant son at home, but I never shared that with Bette. My Aunt Lena, Pop's sister, was always there for me to support me in whatever way I needed and Bette's parents helped too, but their generous efforts didn't necessarily cover me when I had to buy all of the produce for the store and Pop held all of the credit with our vendors at the Hunts Point Market in The Bronx, which had officially opened in 1968 and become the largest wholesale produce market in the world. It didn't matter that I was his son; when Pop informed all of our vendors that I was taking over, he was quick to tell them that "if he doesn't pay you, don't come knocking on my door." That was the one thing I always *did* resent Pop for – leaving me with no credit to buy anything and not standing up for me at the market.

Thankfully, others would soon come to my aid. To this day, I'll never forget the way Harold Katzman, owner of renowned family business S. Katzman Produce and one of the biggest wholesalers at Hunts Point Market, stepped up and took me under his wing. "I know that you're a hard worker and a good guy and I'll tell that to all of the vendors in the market," he assured me. He promised to pay them on my behalf if that was ever necessary, and once he vouched for me, it got easier to buy the produce we needed; without his support, I never would have been able to make it in the produce business. Harold and another colleague, Julius ("Shoey") Rubin of Rubin Brothers Produce, truly helped put me in business and I never took that for granted. I was always diligent about paying everyone back and it's still in my will today to pay the market first and then distribute whatever's left to my kids.

Upon taking over the family store, I cleaned up the space, repainted and installed paneling on the walls, replaced the concrete floors with tile, decorated for each holiday, and made a few other aesthetic changes to make the space look more appealing and the produce more appetizing. I was also very cognizant of the fact that I now had other people – 2-3 year-round employees plus 6-7 part-timers in the summers and at the holidays – and their families depending on me, so I made sure that they were paid every week.

As for my and Bette's family, our son Peter's birth in February 1969 was followed by the birth of our daughter Cheryl in March 1970, just as I was taking over the store. Bette and I had recently bought a house two blocks away from the store in Bergenfield and now utilized the second-floor space over the store – once the apartment where my parents, siblings, and I had lived – for storage and office space. To help meet the needs of both our new business and family, Bette's mother Julie would often watch our kids so that Bette could help me at the store.

Our kids, Peter and Cheryl, during a
holiday season in the early 1970s

For me, taking over our family produce business represented the beginning of many years of hard work, struggle, and 20-hour-a-day, seven-day workweeks. Every night through the 1970s, I would rise at 1:30 or 2 a.m. to go to the Hunts Point Market in The Bronx, load up the truck with everything we needed, and be back in time to set up and open the store by 8 a.m., because in those days many people liked to do their shopping early. For well over a decade, Bette helped handle the bills and she and her friends helped out in the store, but meeting the demands of the business and working side-by-side day in and day out put an occasional strain our marriage. I sometimes took my stress out on Bette, just like my father had on me; though I wasn't as bad as he'd been, I was tired and often blamed her for different situations that weren't her fault. Though we did our best to safeguard family time by keeping the kids with us as much as possible when we went on trips and to restaurants and the kids helped out in the store whenever they wanted, they were usually sleeping by the time I got home each night and I missed out on many of their childhood milestones.

I have more fond memories of those times than bad ones, but running a family operation was tough. Back when my father was the captain of the ship, I remember him telling me that "if there's no money in the register, Petie, we don't eat," so it was engrained in us to always make sure there was money in the till. As I came to learn, that can be especially challenging in the produce business, where margins are very narrow and a decline in volume can cause you to go broke.

To help diversify our business and fill volume gaps, we continued selling seasonal items like Christmas trees and wreaths at the holidays and partnered with local boy scout troops to sell them door-to-door for us. At Halloween, we made trick-or-treat bags with our logo on them to help advertise the store and gave them out to all of the local school kids. By the late 1980s, we also launched a fruit basket business called "Napolitano's Fruit Baskets" with a staff of 3-6 dedicated employees that grew to over 75 during the busy holiday season. Offering a variety of freshly-made baskets filled with everything from apples, pears, grapes, peaches, nectarines, plums, mangoes, pineapples, and other fruits that competing outlets typically wouldn't offer because of their perishability, we were eventually shipping 100-150 fruit, candy, and cheese baskets a day to customers nationwide during the holiday season. The strong demand we experienced was a nice problem to have – within three years, this "side" venture brought in more than our decades-old, bread-and-butter produce business – but we could never get enough help or space to keep up with demand.

We were making money, but the work and lifestyle were hell.

CHAPTER 5

OPPORTUNITY KNOCKS

In the early 1970s, shortly after I'd taken over the business, Bette and I went down to the Jersey shore with the kids during the summer and noticed that new houses were going up along the bay. I remember looking at one in Seaside Park that was priced at $72,000; it would have strained me financially at the time, but I could have stretched and done it. I ended up not buying it, however, because I liked the shore so much and was afraid that the lure of a shore house would cause me to neglect the business. It was an early sign – one of many to come – that I wasn't taking the time to enjoy life.

By the mid-1980s, as I hit my forties, I realized that I'd turned into my father. I couldn't work like this any longer, but our wonderful, loyal customers and the fact that my hard work funded my family's life and enabled me, Bette, and our kids to have nice things motivated me to keep going. While I had a stubbornness and stupidity to think that I could do everything myself and continue working at a breakneck pace, I used to talk about my retirement regularly with Richie Libonati, my and Bette's good friend and owner of Libonati's Tavern (and later "Lib's" restaurant, which featured a legendary Apple Crisp), which had been located next door to our store for decades. As much as Napolitano's Produce had become a driving force in my life, there wasn't a year from 1982 through the mid-1990s, as we'd close up the store for the season every Christmas, that I didn't threaten to shut the doors and not come back the following March. But then I'd go on vacation and get recharged enough to return.

Lib's Amazing Apple Crisp

2 cups Granny Smith apples, peeled and sliced

2 cups Rome apples, peeled and sliced

2 cups flour

2 cups sugar (or less to taste)

2 eggs, beaten

1 teaspoon cinnamon

½ cup (1 stick) unsalted butter, melted

Preheat oven to 350 degrees. Arrange the apples in a baking dish. In a small bowl, mix the flour, sugar, and beaten eggs to crumb consistency with a fork (don't use an electric beater), then sprinkle the crumb mixture over the apples. In a separate bowl, stir the cinnamon into the melted butter and pour over the apple-crumb mixture. Bake for 30-45 minutes, or until the apples are soft and lightly browned. Serve warm with ice cream or whipped cream.

Years earlier, my brother David and I had bought a place in Florida for my parents in their retirement and I assumed I'd do the same – work at the store "until my belly was full," as Pop used to say, and then retire to Florida. That time seemed to be closing in. The physical responsibilities of running the store never bothered me – I'd been used to doing heavy-duty physical labor since I was a kid and could load and unload trucks all day – but the mental part of being a boss and being responsible for the well-being of our employees and their families took a tremendous toll on me. At the same time, as strained as my relationship with my dad was at times, I'd enjoyed seeing and working with my parents every day and I missed their presence there. Working at the store wasn't fun anymore and by the late 1980s, I'd come to the realization that the job was eventually going to end up killing me and that the only way out for me was going to be sideways.

As luck would have it, one winter day in early 1989 a young woman came into our store to buy an apple. I was talking to another customer at the time, but she came up to me and waited until our conversation ended.

"I heard you talking," she said to me. "I work for a local TV show and think you'd make a great segment."

Convinced that she was out of her mind, I completely blew it off and forgot about it. But that March, a fear-inducing, produce-related story made news headlines – two Chilean grapes were reportedly found to be tainted with cyanide and the FDA proceeded to ban the import of all Chilean fruit to the U.S. At the height of this buzz, the woman called me again and asked me if I would come cover this topic on their show. Without hesitation, I once again said no; from my perspective, I was busy running the store and trying to spend the rest of what little window was left of my day at home and had no time to take on anything extra (not to mention that I knew nothing about being on TV). Undeterred, she continued to call several times again over the next 1-2 weeks and one of those times I was out at the market and Bette answered the phone. This time, the woman offered to cover my transportation to and from the studio.

"Sure, he'll do it," decided Bette, who felt that the TV exposure could be good for business and might lead to something else. "Go ahead and send a car for him."

The program was called *People Are Talking* and was a two-hour daily talk show hosted by Renee Hamley and Richard Bey; it was broadcast on WWOR-TV (then channel 9 in the New York/New Jersey area), the same facility Howard Stern was broadcasting from at the time, and was designed to go up against ABC's very popular *Live! with Regis and Kathie Lee* show, which had launched in 1985.

Before the car arrived to take me to the WOR-TV studio in Secaucus, NJ, I asked one of my guys at the store to bring me a box of grapes, which the show hosts later inquired about. During the segment, I explained that there were 20-22 pounds of grapes in a box like the one I had, 4,000 boxes on a tanker, and multiple tankers importing grapes, so it was implausible that someone would find two grapes with cyanide out of hundreds of thousands of pounds of grapes being shipped.

In addition, I shared on-air, "I'm no chemist, but cyanide is an acid and in the three weeks that it would have taken for the grapes to be picked and transported to the U.S., that acidity would have turned those grapes into raisins." I went on to talk a bit about our store and business, and then, right before we went to a commercial break, I nonchalantly popped two grapes from the box into my mouth and ate them. People in our studio audience and on the TV crew suddenly gasped and you could hear a pin drop – after people had been whipped into a frenzy over the dangers of eating Chilean grapes and now feared for their lives if they even *looked* at the fearsome fruit, my act was clearly suicidal.

Later on, Executive Producer Maddie (Rosemary) Henri told me that when we came back on the air, unlike any other time on the show, we hadn't lost one viewer – they were apparently glued to their TV sets to see if I'd dropped dead during the commercial break. I was very much alive and well, however, and Renee and Richard elected to keep me on for the rest of the show after my eight-minute segment ended and kept checking back with me periodically to see if I was alright.

As I got ready to leave the studio after the show, Maddie told me that I was very entertaining and that Bob Woodruff, who ran the whole program and was usually difficult to please, liked my segment and agreed that there was "something there." "Would you like to come back again?" Maddie asked me.

I had to admit, I hadn't been scared to be on TV and had really enjoyed it; it was something fun and different to do, so I accepted her invitation to return.

"Great," she said. "Figure out an item to talk about next week and call me."

I came back to do a segment the following week and then she and Bob took me out to lunch and offered me a paid contract. The Chilean grape scare eventually went away – testing results turned out to be inconclusive and I think that the whole cyanide-tainting fiasco was later determined to have been a hoax – and I would go on to appear on *People Are Talking* once or twice a week from 1989-1992.

I was given the moniker of "Pete Your Produce Pal" on the show, typically wore an apron, and talked about different produce items in season and how to pick and/or prepare them. Response to the segments was strong and an increasing number of viewers sent in self-addressed stamped envelopes (SASEs were how we sent information to fans back in those days) requesting the recipes I shared. And suddenly the store started picking up business we'd never seen before, with people from East Orange and Newark, NJ, Staten Island, NY, and other towns well outside of our immediate vicinity coming into the store and saying "we saw you on TV!"

I did my segments with honesty and transparency, the same way I ran our store; for example, I wouldn't cover anything for advertising reasons or talk about things that weren't in season. Items I discussed had to be in season and readily available to consumers, because plentiful volume would subsequently mean that prices would be reasonable and quality would be high, a reflection of the optimal juncture of supply and demand and the embodiment of my approach to produce.

In terms of media training, the team at *People Are Talking* coached me a little on where to stand during segments and cautioned me to stop moving my hands so much when I spoke (probably a fall-out of my Italian heritage). I also wasn't afraid to ask questions of the producers, find out what I could do differently or better, or take constructive criticism. But I was surprisingly comfortable on air, didn't require a teleprompter, and always looked right into the camera, perhaps a result of having been trained to look people in the eye when I knocked on doors as a kid.

As time went on, I found that doing the show gave me a little room to breathe; I didn't play golf, fish, garden, or engage in any of the other popular hobbies that many other business-people my age turned to in order to relieve job-related stress, so doing the show was recreational for me. It gave me a new view of what was going on in the world and I enjoyed (and was amazed by) the fact that people would take time out of their day to come up to me and say hi, shake my hand, and tell me that they appreciated what I did. Back at Napolitano's Produce, I found that my employees could unload trucks, sweep floors, etc.

and that the store still ran 24/7 without my constant oversight and involvement.

Over the three-year period that I did weekly segments at WOR-TV, the show changed up a few times. Richard Bey was let go as the show's male anchor in 1990/1991 and, in an attempt to freshen up the format and attract new and more viewers, management changed the show's title to *9 Broadcast Plaza* and debuted a new three-hour news program that aired from 9 a.m.-12 noon each day. They brought in a couple of different co-hosts, one of whom was a talented young broadcaster named Matt Lauer (who eventually left for another opportunity), and did away with all of the old show's featured segments (they'd previously had regular segments with a fisherman, mechanic, etc.) except for mine, because my viewership numbers were so strong.

Me standing in front of our store in the early 1990s, when I was doing weekly segments on WWOR-TV's "People Are Talking" as 'Pete Your Produce Pal'

Six months later, in late 1991, when this new format failed to drive the surge in ratings they'd hoped for, they brought back Richard Bey and launched a new program called *The Richard Bey Show*. While I liked doing the show, it started to become sensational like *The Jerry Springer Show*; I'd be sharing my usual tips about oranges or apples after segments featuring cheerleaders in skimpy tops or guests talking about "why my grandmother keeps having sex with my friends."

By the summer of 1992, the format wasn't fun for me and doing the show didn't feel right anymore. I was 47 and it wasn't my day job; I always knew that if I didn't want to do the show any longer or if I felt it would embarrass me or my family, I'd just say no, so I informed the show's management that I wanted to leave. On my last segment on the show, to my surprise, confetti fell from the ceiling, "Auld Lang Syne" played, and anchorwoman Renee Hamley informed viewers that it was my last show and that I'd be returning to running my family business.

That was on a Wednesday.

The next day (Thursday), I received a call from Matt Lauer, whom I'd met during our *9 Broadcast Plaza* days. He'd just gotten a job as co-anchor of WNBC's *Today in New York* with McGee Hickey and informed me that the station was going to be starting a new weekend show on Saturdays with segments. "I suggested you as one of them," Matt told me. Though I assured him that I wasn't interested, he said that I should go in for an audition.

I took his advice and went in to WNBC for an audition that Friday. In the interview, I was honest and just tried to be myself; I remember displaying a bunch of Brussels sprouts and saying something like, "honey, I shrunk the cabbage!", which made everybody laugh. I just went for it and didn't take it too seriously. Three other guys, all of whom were actors, also tried out for the slot, but I ended up getting the job and WNBC started me on *Weekend Today in New York* at 6 a.m. the very next day!

During the time that Matt was anchor of *Today in New York*, everyone could see that he was really good; no one was surprised when he eventually got tapped to anchor the national edition of *Today*. We remained friendly for years and he was instrumental in my career, helping me get a little "in" to an opportunity that would completely change my life.

CHAPTER 6

LUCKY BREAK

When I was growing up, my mom was very handy and always made everything for us, including our Halloween costumes. When I was about 8 or 9 and we lived in Tenafly, she came up with a funny idea for my costume that year – using a box that she got at a store, she crafted a TV around my upper body with my face as the screen.

"See, Petie," Mom gushed, "you're on TV!"

"Geez, I'd love to be on TV," I remember telling her, though I never thought in a million years that it would or could ever happen.

WNBC changed my life forever and was my lucky break. Sometimes I still can't believe the stroke of luck that landed me the media opportunities I've been given or the factors that have continued to sustain me on TV for three decades. I've been on TV for longer than I had my store, which is amazing to me. I've been involved with TV for nearly half of my life – the very best half – and I feel like the luckiest guy in the world. Being in front of the camera has always come naturally to me and I've never been nervous; I just try to be myself, share my honest opinions, help people better understand products that I've worked with my whole life, and keep things simple. I've been very careful about what I say on the air and post on Twitter and Facebook because I know that spoken or written words are indelible. I care about my public image and feel that I owe it to the public, who see me as a friend, as well as to the WNBC network, which bestowed on me a golden opportunity and a different life, and to my family to always be appropriate and respectful.

I've never taken my opportunity for granted; in fact, in the fast-moving TV environment, where celebrities are routinely told "you're great!" one day and "you're fired!" the next, I've always felt that my situation could be taken away from me at any time. WNBC *Weekend Today in New York* news anchor Pat Battle, who's a great friend of mine, once told me that I've always behaved like the other shoe was going to fall every day. When network executives have called me upstairs, however, I'm happy to say that it was to tell me that I was doing a good job, not the opposite, and I take a lot of pride in that.

In the over 30 years since my first appearance on *Weekend Today in New York* in September 1992, a number of things have changed on my segments.

Among them, our show has featured a variety of different and wonderful hosts and meteorologists over the years, from

David Ushery, Darlene Rodriguez, Chris Cimino, Janice Huff, Bill Boggs, Michael Gargiulo, Peri Peltz, and Jen Maxfield to our current news anchors, Pat Battle and Gus Rosendale, and meteorologist Raphael Miranda; I've enjoyed working with and learning from each and every one of them. We've filmed in three or four different studios over the decades and our set designs have been updated to remain fresh and modern. My name in the segments has evolved from "Pete Your Produce Pal" in the early years to "Produce Pete" today, while the time of my segment on Saturdays has moved from the 6 a.m. hour to the more popular 8 a.m. or 9 a.m. hours based on the strong fan following and viewership I've been lucky to amass.

Bette and me with WNBC Weekend Today in
New York anchors and crew members

Based on their popularity over the years, I've done more and more "field" and "in-store" segments on the show, going on location to different farms or retail outlets to show viewers how tomatoes, eggplants, pumpkins, or Christmas trees are grown, what the new varieties of apple trees look like, how different produce items are priced and transported to markets nationwide, and how to select a variety of products. Years back, the overwhelming majority of my segments were done live in the studio and maybe only two or three a year were filmed on location out in the field; just prior to the COVID-19 pandemic, nearly half of my annual 52 segments were shot on location, as viewers have responded positively to these educational visits to farms, farmer's markets, and stores in an attempt to bring the public closer to the source of their food.

The format of my segments has also evolved over the years. I used to come on and introduce a produce item, demonstrate how to select it, and then share a recipe, but now I lead with a personal story or recollection from my life that relates to that produce item. This happened naturally out of my habit of speaking honestly and off the cuff. I'll never forget one of the first stories I told on the show; we were doing a segment on pomegranates and I shared that when I was a kid, I thought that eating pomegranates made your teeth fall out, a statement which elicited an on-air look of shock from Pat Battle.

"What?!" she laughed in disbelief.

I explained to her and our viewers that whenever my uncles ate pomegranates, they'd take their teeth out; I later came to understand that they were removing their dentures to tackle this challenging, seeded fruit. It was such an entertaining and honest bit of nostalgia that from that point on, Pat suggested that I talk more about my family and memories because those types of stories were funny, real, and resonated with viewers.

Another thing that's changed over time are the viewers themselves. In past years, my audience was typically comprised of women in their 50s, 60s, and 70s. Today, more and more of my viewers are millennial women (and men) in their 20s and 30s who watch me while working out at home or in the gym on Saturday morning and are interested in eating healthy foods like fresh and local produce. The women increasingly work and don't necessarily have the time or experience in the kitchen that my mother's or wife's generations logged, so it's new to them and they learn from cooking shows and segments like mine.

One thing that *hasn't* changed over the years is my gratitude for the opportunity to be Produce Pete. I love what I do and I do it for the wonderful fans, who are like family to me. It's incredibly flattering to have people come up to you and shake your hand or tell you that they love what you do, especially when you were told your whole life that you were a bum and would never amount to anything.

I remember one day when I was young and working at the store, my father and I happened to watch as a Bell Telephone worker came out of Libonati's Tavern next door, went to his work truck, handed another guy a phone, and accepted $5 for it. Pop was rattled by the exchange and immediately saw it as a teaching moment.

"See that, Petie? For $5, he's willing to lose his job," he said to me about the incident, in which the Bell worker clearly stole the phone from his company, sold it privately, and pocketed the gain.

While I'm no saint, I learned from Pop at an early age to do the right thing, know where your bread is buttered, and not kill the golden goose. For that reason, I've never taken anything for free from any vendors and I've always been open with the management at WNBC about any other media opportunities I've been offered in order to be transparent and ensure that there was no conflict.

And opportunities came rolling in. As a result of my segments on WNBC and even before that while I was on *People Are Talking/9 Broadcast Plaza/The Richard Bey Show*, I was invited to be on other programs. In 1990, two years prior to joining *WNBC Weekend Today in New York*, for instance, I was invited to be on WNBC's *House Party*, a weekday show hosted by Steve Doocy that featured comedic home-related situations. They originally asked me to play the role of "Pete the Prince of Produce" on the show and sport an English accent, which I flat out refused to do; the word "no" was probably something the producer wasn't used to hearing, but they didn't press me on it.

If I'd seen this as my "career," I might have done more of what people wanted me to do – look a certain way, change my manner of speaking, etc. Some people listen to others who steer them in a wrong or uncomfortable direction because they have no other choice – e.g., "you either do this or you're out." But I didn't perceive it as my career. I already had a house, a second home in Florida, kids in college, and a business. I wasn't a rich guy, but I had a life, and that grounding drove a lot of my choices and decisions.

In one episode of *House Party*, they flew in a guy who could catch grapes in his mouth from 30-40 feet away and had me drop grapes to him from the fifth floor of a building. It was a fun experience that was filmed on the Saturday Night Live stage in Manhattan.

Other shows I appeared on included a 1995 Discovery Channel episode of *Home Matters*, a 1997 WNBC episode of *Steals and Deals*, a 2000 episode of *Woman's Home Network* with Joan Lunden, and weekly episodes of WNBC's *Ainsley Harriott Show*, a series launched in 2000 that was hosted by Ainsley, a wonderful English chef, and executive produced by Merv Griffin (whom I got to meet at the wrap party). I was also on *The View* in 2004 with co-hosts Barbara Walters, Rosie O'Donnell, and Joy Behar, the national *Today* show in 2006, the *Italian American Network* in 2007, and *The Dr. Oz Show* in 2014 and 2015 in addition to numerous radio spots, speaking appearances, and spokesperson gigs.

On the Dr. Oz Show 7-8 years ago

Doing a radio show with friend and writer/co-author Susan Bloom in 2014

Another couple of interesting opportunities came my way as a result of my segment on WNBC. One was my partnership with Pathmark stores.

In 2000, Bette was working as the administrative assistant to the president of Konica in Ramsey, NJ. Jim Donald was the CEO of Pathmark, which bought its store-brand film from Konica. One day Jim came to Konica for a meeting with Bette's boss and, after greeting Bette, happened to notice my picture on her desk.

"Wow…do you know him?" Jim asked Bette.

"Yeah, I know him," Bette laughed. "I'm *married* to him!"

At home later, Bette relayed this story to me and that Jim said he wanted to meet me, which I assumed was because he wanted Pathmark to get some kind of representation on my WNBC segments. Bette set up a meeting between Jim and me at Pathmark's headquarters in Carteret, NJ and I soon learned that they were actually interested in *my* representation.

"Come work for us at Pathmark," he said.

Being the honest guy that I am, I shared the truth. "Bette and I have shopped at the Pathmark in our town for decades," I told him, "but your produce isn't always the best."

"You're right," Jim conceded, "but you could fix it."

He wanted me to not only be a face of Pathmark but to tell his people what they were doing wrong and advise them on how and when items should be set up, promoted, etc.

I didn't necessarily want the job, but, like a scene out of a movie, he wrote a number down on a piece of paper and pushed it across the table to me. It was a huge offer. Convinced that my dad, who passed away in 1998, was looking down on me and would say to do it, I signed a one-year contract and became a spokesperson for Pathmark. At the time, Pathmark had 143 stores throughout New York, New Jersey, Pennsylvania, and Delaware and most were doing well. As a spokesperson, my picture and 'pick of the week' appeared in the chain's weekly flyers and sales of that item would typically increase by 30-40% that week. In addition to working with store produce managers, who all liked me, I traveled 100,000 miles a year to make personal appearances at different Pathmark stores each weekend, typically hitting stores in Pennsylvania and Delaware on Fridays when I had more time and more local New York and New Jersey branches on Saturdays after my segment on WNBC. I'd do demonstrations involving each pick of the week, showing customers how to select and prepare pineapples, peaches, plums, etc., and then cut them up and serve them with toothpicks, which would often draw crowds of shoppers.

I also did about 5-6 TV commercials for Pathmark each year, some of which Pathmark elected to run after my WNBC segment because viewership was high. I was very up-front with WNBC about the job from the beginning and assured them that, to avoid any conflicts of interest, I wouldn't be covering Pathmark's 'Pick of the Week' during my Saturday segments.

Doing a demonstration in a supermarket in the early 2000s

My original one-year stint with Pathmark lasted from 2001 until 2010, when Pathmark filed for bankruptcy. Pathmark was subsequently purchased by A&P; I worked for A&P for six months and quit, and then A&P filed for bankruptcy the following year. The closure of renowned, long-standing supermarket chains like Pathmark, A&P, Fairway Market, and others has been an unfortunate trend today and I think comes back to management teams that weren't in touch with what the public wanted – the truth and someone they can talk to. Many of those supermarkets erroneously – and fatally – believed that they were the ones in control and didn't want to hear input from customers. As the owner of a nearly 50-year-old, family-run produce business that always went above and beyond to take care of its customers, the truth is that the customer – the one coming in with the shopping cart – is the one who should control what you do.

One other opportunity I pursued was with S. Katzman Produce. As a leading, 100+-year-old, fourth-generation wholesaler/distributor of quality produce at the Hunts Point Market, my dad and I regularly bought from the Katzmans and they'd become like family. After I retired from our store in 1997, a few industry players began calling me about brokering for them – e.g., helping to connect produce buyers with sellers and negotiate terms and agreements – but I held off. When patriarch Harold Katzman got sick in 1999-2000 and asked me to work with his son Stephen, however, I jumped at the opportunity to help support Steve and his team by brokering, buying products, filing, and doing whatever else they needed.

I'd known Steve, who was 11 years younger than me, since he was a kid and had always found him to be a terrific person and smart businessman. Though I thought I'd only be helping out for a couple of months, I've worked about three days a week for them for the past 20+ years and it's been a fantastic two decades. Located at their headquarters in The Bronx, I take care of local stores like Sickles Market, Stew Leonard's, and certain other customers, broker some products from farmers, review files, and address any customer issues and I'm proud to be part of the outstanding S. Katzman team.

Me with supermarket mogul Stew Leonard and
Stephen Katzman, President of S. Katzman Produce

CHAPTER 7

FAMILY MATTERS

They say that hard work will never kill you, but working in our store seven days a week the way I did, even with the happy distraction of my TV segments, definitely would have. In 1997, I officially "retired" from the store and relocated to the house we'd bought in Florida, a lifestyle choice my dad had made and one which I thought I wanted too. For about six months, I'd fly home to New Jersey every Friday night to do *NBC Weekend Today in New York* on Saturday morning and then fly back down to Florida on Saturday afternoon once it was over; Bette was still working in New Jersey and would fly down to join me on the weekends. However, I soon found out that the whole retirement thing didn't work for me – I couldn't sit on a beach, read a book, and watch seagulls. I liked living in New Jersey, doing my TV segments, and pursuing the other media opportunities that were increasingly coming my way.

Upon my retirement in 1997, I gave the business – whose name we changed from "Napolitano's Produce" to "Produce Pete's

Fruit Baskets" in 1998/1999 – to my son Peter. He was a college graduate, had worked at the store for years, and thought he'd do it forever. He successfully operated the business from 1997-2006, but as a married man with kids of his own, he didn't like the hours, felt he never saw his family, and ultimately decided he didn't want to run it anymore. I couldn't blame him; unlike my father, who'd raised me for the business, I raised Peter to be my son and his comfort and happiness were paramount. In 2006, after 47 years in operation (and several years before that at previous locations), we officially closed the store in Bergenfield. I decided not to sell the business because, now that I was on TV, I didn't feel confident that I'd be able to control the use of my name, and I certainly didn't want to go back to running it in any way. It was time for a change.

Every winter after my parents retired to Florida in the early 1970s, Bette and I would take our kids down there to visit their grandparents; for the first few years, we'd also see my sister LuAnne, who lived with them until she left for college. LuAnne was about 12 when Mom and Pop moved down south with her and she ended up attending junior high and high school in the Sunshine State. Spared of the hard-scrabble upbringing and long work hours that my brother and I had endured as kids to help support the family business, she ended up having a very different childhood than David and I did. In addition, since I was 14 when LuAnne was born, my sister only ever knew me with Bette and Bette was always a part of her life.

Once my parents were down in Florida, I'll never forget how every St. Patrick's Day, my hardcore Italian father would dress up in a green sport jacket, green pants, and a green tie, get on the motorcycle he'd bought, pick up the Irish nuns at LuAnne's Catholic school, and ride them in the St. Patrick's Day Parade in Delray. Growing up, our whole family loved and looked forward to a meal of Mom's classic corned beef and cabbage with red potatoes every St. Patrick's Day (even though Pop wanted to put tomato sauce on it). I guess the old saying that everyone is Irish on St. Patty's Day is really true!

Louise Napolitano's "Lucky" Corned Beef and Cabbage

3 pounds corned beef brisket with spice packet

8-10 small red potatoes, cut in half

5 carrots, peeled and cut into 3-inch pieces

1 large head green cabbage, cut into wedges

Place corned beef in large pot or Dutch oven and cover with water. Add the spice packet that came with the corned beef. Cover pot and bring to a boil, then reduce to a simmer for approximately 45 minutes per pound or until fork tender. Add potatoes and carrots and cook until the vegetables are almost tender. Add cabbage and cook for 10-15 more minutes. Remove meat and let rest 15 minutes. Slice meat across the grain, serve with carrots, potatoes, and cabbage, and enjoy!

*Pop on his motorcycle (with mom behind him!) all decked out in green
during the St. Patrick's Day parade in Delray Beach, FL in March 1973*

My mom had always been very social and at one point I remember her getting a part-time job driving a tram for elderly resi-
dents at a Century Village complex. During one of our visits, she
brought my young son Peter on the tram with her one day and
boasted to me later that he'd been so funny and innocent, asking the elderly riders in the back what Santa Claus had brought
them for Christmas that year. Mom was very friendly, enjoyed
talking to people, and loved being a grandmother. Pop knew
how to order and price products, but Mom truly fueled our
family business and there never would have been a Napolitano's
Produce without her. I was excited that my mom had gotten to
see me on TV in 1989 because *People Are Talking* was a national
show that was televised in their area.

After I took over the store in 1970 and my parents moved to Florida, Mom would call me at the store every day at noon just to say hi. One day in March 1990 she called me and was slurring her words a bit. I told my father to take her to the hospital immediately, but it was too late; she'd suffered a stroke and lapsed into a coma from which she never recovered. My brother, sister, and I flew down to Florida during those last difficult days and brought her back to New Jersey for the funeral. For me, it was extremely tough to lose my beloved mom and co-worker, a great woman who loved us unconditionally, made us kids believe there was nothing we couldn't do, and kept the whole family together with her industriousness and upbeat spirit, even in difficult times.

Mom and Pop in the 1970s

After Mom passed, hundreds of people showed up at her wake, including a ton of customers, and it meant everything to me to see how much they loved her and cared about our family. After the funeral, my brother David and I went back to Florida with my dad to help get him settled into his condo and ready to face a "new normal" without Mom. I'll never forget how at one point during our ride, Pop broke down crying in the back seat. David and I were shocked and confused; he wasn't an emotional guy and I'd never seen him cry, even at Mom's funeral or wake, but David and I chalked it up to Pop finally realizing what he'd had – and lost.

In the early 1990s, I got a letter from an editor at William Morrow who said that he enjoyed my segments on TV and wanted to know if I'd be interested in doing a book. I didn't think I could do it, but the publisher paired me up with a ghost writer to help me and gave me a big advance. The book, called *Produce Pete's Farmacopeia*, was a black and white collection of tips and recipes on produce items "from apples to zucchini and everything in between" and came out in 1994. As a relative unknown, I was happy with it. The publisher arranged for me to do TV and radio interviews all over the country to promote the book and it sold over 20,000 copies. Several years later, I bought the rights back, self-published it, and have since sold another 20,000-30,000 copies on my own.

A promotional shot taken for my book, Produce Pete's Farmacopeia, in 1994

At a book signing in the 1990s

Pop found my book interesting because he saw it as something that left a legacy, and although it was always hard for him to praise me or ever say "good job" for anything, I think he enjoyed me on TV too. I brought Pop onto *People Are Talking* with me once. I remember that we were doing a segment on broccoli rabe, a staple in my dad's diet when he was growing up because it was inexpensive, and host Renee Hamley said to him, "so, Mr. Napolitano, what do you think of your son?" To which Pop replied on the air, "why didn't you have *me* on? I'm the original!" Later, after tasting the tasty broccoli rabe recipe that Bette had prepared for the segment, he told Renee, "it's good, but the stems are a little stringy." As someone who was so appreciative of everything I had, Pop's never-satisfied attitude drove me crazy sometimes. He was someone who, if he won money for hitting five out of six numbers on a lottery ticket, would be mad because he hadn't hit the sixth number and won the big pot.

Grandma Albertelli's Famous Broccoli Rabe Pie

Made by the grandmother of close family friends of ours (the Schembri family), I showed this pie on Weekend Today in New York years ago and thousands of fans have since requested the recipe from me. My Pop was a big fan of dishes with broccoli rabe, so this one's for him!)

(Note: mixture should be dry)

1 pound broccoli rabe, cleaned

1 onion, medium dice

2 garlic cloves, sliced thin

½ pound sausage, no casing

½ pound ricotta cheese (whole milk)

½ pound mozzarella cheese, shredded

¼ cup grated parmesan cheese

3 eggs, beaten

2 frozen deep-dish pie crust shells

2 tablespoons olive oil

Remove two pie shells from freezer. When thawed, remove one pie shell from its aluminum pan and place on wax paper; keep the second crust in the pan. Steam or boil broccoli rabe briefly, then sauté with garlic and oil. Strain the broccoli rabe and garlic mixture to remove the excess liquid. Chop the mixture finely and move aside for later use. Cook the sausage and the diced onions fully, making sure everything is finely chopped, without any large pieces of meat, then drain off any excess liquid. Add sausage mixture to the broccoli rabe mixture and blend well. Next, add the ricotta, the mozzarella, and the grated parmesan cheese, and then add the beaten eggs. Mix everything well.

Add the warm broccoli rabe and sausage mixture to the pie crust and distribute evenly. Add flattened pie crust shell to the top. Cut a vent hole in the center of the pie and pinch the edges of the two crusts together. Brush the top of the pie and the edges with a beaten egg yolk. Place pie on a cookie sheet and bake at 375 degrees for 45-60 minutes or until golden brown. Let sit for 15 minutes before serving.

Me at home displaying a freshly-made broccoli rabe pie

While my parents retired to Florida, Bette's parents retired to Yucca Valley, CA in 1979. Bette's mom Julie loved California and her son (and Bette's older brother) Donnie, a major in the Marine Corp, lived there with his wife and kids and Julie was excited to be closer to them. Tragically, Julie suffered a stroke in 1985 at the age of 67 and lived in a nursing home for the next 11 years; Bette's father Bucky visited her there every day. When she passed in 1996, our family held her funeral in California and then flew her body back to New Jersey for another funeral and burial at Mt. Carmel Cemetery in Tenafly. Bucky died in 1998 and was buried alongside his wife.

My father died of lung cancer in 1998, at the age of 78. As Pop was dying, I brought him from Florida back north to Rosary Hill Home, a hospice in Westchester County, NY. I visited him there every day with my grandson Griffin, whom Pop would always hold on his lap for a while. Pop always felt cold in his room and one day I remember getting him a blanket and arranging it around him.

He looked up at me and said quietly, "I never thought you'd do that for me."

I looked back at my hard-working, stoic father who'd been a towering presence all my life, now weak and in his final days. "Neither did I," I responded. It was a bittersweet moment I'll never forget.

I loved my mom and was a real mama's boy, but to this day I still dream about the store and my father every night, even when he was yelling at me, and I miss him more than any of my other relatives. I gave the eulogy at his funeral and was very honest about who he was.

"Your father is a tough man to love," my mom used to tell me. There was a time when my father and I didn't talk for months and I thought I hated him, but the truth is that I'll love him to the day I die.

CHAPTER 8

FANS FIRST

Up until my mid-40s, I was Pete Napolitano. Since then, I've been "Produce Pete." I'm the same guy, but in a way I'm two separate people. In the beginning, it was strange for me to get recognized at different places I went throughout the tri-state area, but I've gotten used to it. I used to be bombarded for autograph requests, but no one asks for autographs anymore; now it's all cell phone selfies – people just want to take a picture with me.

I'm not going to say that having a bit of local "celebrity" hasn't come with its share of perks over the years. I've gotten past crowds in restaurants without reservations, chefs will often come out to say hello to me if they hear I'm in the restaurant, and one holiday season our family was standing on a mile-long line waiting to ice skate at Rockefeller Center in New York City and the guard opened the gate for me and let us right through, which my kids loved. Another evening, Bette and I were enjoying frozen drinks at a restaurant at the Jersey Shore and a ton of people came up to us to say hello, which was very nice.

Bette and I in the early 2000s

While all of that would make anyone feel good, I was definitely uncomfortable with the attention at first and still don't understand why some people get nervous when meeting me or why they're trembling when we shake hands, because I'm just Pete. Most fans are incredibly gracious and, out of fear that they're invading my space or intruding on my free time, will approach me by first saying "I'm so sorry to bother you." I always thank them for saying hi and tell them that it's no bother at all; if I wasn't so lucky to be doing what I do, they wouldn't know who I was. The fact that they even know who I am is the reflection of a dream come true.

That's not to say that I haven't had some strange, funny, or memorable fan encounters in the last three decades, however.

Years ago, Bette and I were having dinner at a restaurant in Fort Lee, NJ and a woman at the next table kept looking over at us, so I finally just turned to her and said hi. She was so excited about what she perceived as an "invitation" to join us that she proceeded to leave her husband sitting alone, move her chair over to our table, and start sharing our tiramisu with us! More recently, I went on a radio program on behalf of a restaurant magazine and then participated in a dinner event in north Jersey afterwards. A female attendee started talking to me during dinner, asking my secret to a long marriage, and then began sharing lurid details of her own recent divorce and current sex life; editors around me were all rolling their eyes my way in shock, embarrassment, and in sympathy for the fact that I was a total captive trapped in an incredibly uncomfortable situation.

As a function of people generally being very nice and happy to meet you, they also think that they know you or that you're their long-lost cousin because they've watched you on TV for years, which is actually as flattering as it gets. Still, I've been amazed at some of the personal things fans notice and reach out to me about by e-mail or on the street, such as when they compliment me on a particular sweater, a different watch, or a new wedding band I wore on TV. One Saturday, I was out sick and a lot of fans reached out to ask me where I was. Twenty years ago, fans also reached out to me with concern following the birth of my twin grandkids Alexandra and Zachary, who were born prematurely and evacuated to a hospital by helicopter. (They're both all grown up now and doing great, by the way)!

I get a lot of e-mails from fans who say very nice things and even send me thank-you notes for merchandise they purchased on my website (I sell my book, *Produce Pete's Farmacopeia*, as well as Produce Pete-branded aprons, reusable grocery bags, and oven mitts). Over the years, some have even sent me incredibly sentimental offerings. One year a fan knitted and shipped me a beautiful Christmas sweater, which must have taken her months to complete but which I've truly enjoyed wearing every holiday season. And I'll never forget the time about 10 or 12 years ago when I made an appearance at a

I received this beautiful handmade sweater from a fan and take pride in wearing it every holiday season

Pathmark store in Ramsey, NJ and an elderly lady handed me an envelope with my mother's distinctive handwriting on it. It turned out that the lady had been a friend of my mother's in the early 1940s and was giving me a letter that my mother had written to her, postmarked from 1944, sharing how much she missed my father while he was serving overseas in WWII. It was so unexpected and special to me that I immediately framed it and hung it on a wall in our house.

Some of the pictures I've taken with fans over the years have stood out. I was once in a restaurant in Nyack, NY with friends from Florida when a group of young girls attending a bachelorette party came in. Someone in the group recognized me and eventually one of the girls came over and said that her friends wanted pictures with me. They were very nice and the bride-to-be later e-mailed me to say that she'd shared our pictures at their wedding and included them in her wedding album. It's fun and touching when these pictures become so meaningful and people think enough of you to do that. Another time, a 21-year-old girl came up to me to ask for a "follow-up" picture; she then showed me a picture I'd taken with her mother and herself – then a one-year-old baby in her mom's arms – two decades earlier. I love that in some small way I can be part of the lives of multiple generations.

Being recognized somewhere can sometimes be tricky, particularly when you're trying to eat or if you're not feeling well, but most fans are very nice and some of them are very funny too. For instance, I remember being in the supermarket with Bette one day when a woman accidentally hit the front of my cart.

Her eyes lit up as she recognized me. "You don't remember me, do you?" she asked.

I looked her up and down trying to figure out where I might have known her from – was she someone from my childhood, a friend's wife or sister, or a member of my own extended family? – but I kept drawing a blank. "I'm sorry," I told her. "I don't."

"That's because I'm always in my nightgown when you see me," she said.

"Whoa!" I said, confused and nervous that Bette would get the wrong idea.

"No worries," she smiled. "That's just what I'm wearing when I watch you every Saturday morning!" We all laughed at her creative ice-breaker.

Some encounters can be heartbreaking, like when people ask me to sign something for their dying mother. In other cases, fans will often ask me to get on the phone with a friend or relative who's a fan. I'll never forget one time when I was driving to an Italian American Club event and was running late; I must have been hitting the gas pedal a little too hard because a cop turned on his lights behind me and pulled me over for speeding.

He recognized me immediately as soon as I rolled down my window. "Are you Produce Pete?" he asked. "My wife loves you!"

He immediately grabbed his cell phone, dialed his wife, and asked me to say hello to her. Since I always kept copies of my book in the car with me, I told her that her husband had pulled me over, but I thanked her for being a fan and promised to give him an autographed book to bring home to her. The cop thanked me, then asked for my license and registration and walked back to his car. I was positive that I'd beaten a ticket, but no such luck – sure enough, he walked right back to my car and handed me a summons like our previous exchange had never happened! I didn't get mad, though – the way I saw it, he was just doing his job, and I was doing mine by greeting a fan.

Though most fans typically come up to *me* with questions, I've picked up some interesting tips from them over the years as well. A woman once told me that she removes dirt from her spinach by putting it in the washing machine – essentially a high-tech salad spinner! Another woman who grew her own tomatoes once shared with me that at the end of the season, before the first frost occurs, she'd take any green tomatoes still growing on the vine, wrap them in newspaper, and put them in the basement to successfully ripen them.

Sometimes my fans have been celebrities themselves, which has never failed to amaze me. Comedian and actor Steve Carell did a funny series of segments spoofing me on *Comedy Central's "The Daily Show"* from 2002-2005 and the legendary Robert DeNiro once did a great send-up on me in a 2010 *Saturday Night Live* sketch. Actor Mandy Patinkin came on *Weekend Today in New York* once and was extremely gracious, urging me to continue to be myself and stay grounded, explaining that "being famous only means being seen more." I often ran into late actor Danny Aiello at the cemetery in New Jersey when I was visiting my mother's grave and he was visiting a deceased relative of his own. I recently met one of my own childhood idols, radio personality Bruce ("Cousin Brucie") Morrow, who informed me that he'd been a fan of mine for a long time (incredible!), and, while working on the WNBC show *House Party* in 1990, celebrity chef Emeril Lagasse once brought me up to sit at a chair at the counter during his cooking demo.

When actor Blair Underwood came on *Weekend Today in New York* in 1992, I remember him asking me a number of questions because he was just starting out. And when Donny Osmond appeared on the show and we got to talking, I got the chance to tell him that he'd practically been part of the Napolitano family because my daughter Cheryl had posters of him all over her room when she was growing up, which made him laugh.

I met celebrity gossip columnist Cindy Adams when she used to do regular segments on *WNBC Weekend Today in New York*, and, despite the obvious difference in the circles we ran in, we got along great and she'd often ask me for advice on how to prepare different fruits and vegetables at home. One time, I gave her some produce in a shopping bag with the Produce Pete logo on it that I'd made especially for her and she loved it; that's actually how I got the idea to begin selling them to the public. I'll never forget attending a dinner party that she threw one night and being elbow-to-elbow with top editors, socialites, and even Shirley MacLaine. I remember looking around and asking Cindy, "why do you want *me* here?" And she said, "because you're interesting!"

Hanging out with renowned gossip columnist and friend
Cindy Adams, whom I met on NBC "Weekend Today in New York"

I also remember meeting Harrison Ford when we both appeared on *The View* in 2004. "Hey, Produce Pete!" he shouted to me across the green room.

I was shocked and blown away by his acknowledgement and warm greeting. "Wow!" I said. I know *you*, but how the hell do you know *me*?"

I've never really understood the recognition and attention. Back when I was doing weekend appearances at Pathmark stores as their spokesperson, hundreds of fans would show up at a particular store on a Friday or Saturday just to say hello to me and enjoy some of the produce I was sampling that day; sometimes the store had to bring a cop onsite to manage the crowds and traffic. For a number of years (pre-pandemic), I took part in the annual *NBC 4 New York and Telemundo 47 Health & Fitness Expo* at MetLife Stadium in East Rutherford, NJ and crowds of people stood on line for up to two hours to meet me; during the 2019 iteration of this event, I took pictures with 4,000 eager fans in one day. And at appearances I've made at local festivals and farmers' markets all over New Jersey and New York, I've often been greeted by large crowds of people awaiting my arrival.

I'm still amazed when I show up somewhere and a crowd of people has congregated, because whenever I see a crowd, I wonder, "who's here?" The attention is extremely flattering, but I've always tried to avoid taking it too seriously or letting it go to my head. My kids and grandkids have enjoyed it over the years, but to me and my wife and friends, I'm still Pete Napolitano, not Produce Pete. Celebrity happened to me later in life, which was a great thing because I was able to stay grounded. I never looked at myself as being famous, but rather just a guy who was able to communicate with people, share information and stories, and help people tap into memories and nostalgia from their own lives. Ninety percent of people who come up to me greet me by saying that they saw me on TV demonstrating a particular produce item and that "my mother (or grandmother) used to do that too!"

*Working the NBC 4 New York and Telemundo 47 Health &
Fitness Expo desk at MetLife Stadium in East Rutherford,
NJ in 2019 with news anchors Pat Battle and Gus Rosendale*

You might wonder how my wife has responded to all of the fan
attention over the years, since she's been with me when a lot of it
occurs and it affects her life too. Bette is used to it and has generally been very supportive, though she's protective of me as well
and often gets offended if people say negative things about my
broadcast, perspectives, or personal traits, which they sometimes

do. I don't take any of that personally, though. Pop always used to say that you can't make someone like you, so I never let one person's opinion bother me.

Instead, I feel grateful for the attention, because it changed my life. I came from nothing and worked like a dog for decades. Getting the chance to be on TV and be able to take care of my family with my voice and personality instead of my physical braun saved my life; without that opportunity, I'm sure I would have toiled in that store for decades more and eventually dropped dead there. The way I see it, it's a heck of a lot harder to load or unload a truck than to stop and say hi to a fan. So if you ever see me on the street, don't hesitate to come up and say hello – it's my honor and privilege to meet you!

CHAPTER 9

BEHIND THE SCENES

As you can imagine, after more than 30 years on TV, I've had my share of funny interactions, flubs, and memorable experiences.

I remember one laughable situation that happened about 20 years ago when I was filming a field segment for WNBC at a Fairway supermarket on Broadway in Manhattan. Currently, there's ordinarily only one crew member working the camera at these types of shoots, but back then there were many, many more. I was preparing to wrap up our piece on pineapples when an elderly lady, clearly oblivious to all of the cameras, walked into our frame, got right in my face, and asked, "where's the milk?!" She obviously thought I was a clerk there. I laughed and the footage ended up being so funny and unique that the producer kept it in the files.

Before doing my segments on WNBC, the crew always helps me set up my produce display on a table and wheel it out onto the set. One time, we'd just gone live when cantaloupes started rolling off my table. A crew member ran out into the frame to grab them and later said to me, "well, I guess I got my five minutes of fame!"

During one WNBC episode that I did on strawberries with Matt Lauer, Matt brought Bette on with a dish she'd made – pears with strawberry sauce – that featured the segment's spotlight fruit. When he asked her to describe to viewers what she'd brought, she said, "I made pears with tomato sauce!" to which Matt laughed and said *"what?!"* Poor Bette was nervous and embarrassed, but it was funny.

Bette's Bartlett Pears with Strawberry (not Tomato!) Sauce

(makes 6 servings)

6 Bartlett pears, peeled but with stem and base left intact

¾ cup water

1 teaspoon lemon juice

½ cup sugar

Strawberry sauce

For the Strawberry Sauce:

2 cups fresh (or frozen, thawed) strawberries, washed and hulled

¼ cup water

¼ cup sugar

1 tablespoon lemon juice

3 tablespoon cornstarch

1/3 cup brandy (optional)

Place the strawberries in a medium-sized saucepan, add the water, sugar, and lemon juice, and bring to a boil over moderate heat. When the strawberries are soft, remove from heat and allow to cool slightly. Pour the mixture into a blender or food processor and purée until smooth. Strain through a sieve, then return the mixture to the saucepan. Gradually stir in the cornstarch and brandy (optional), and cook over low heat, stirring constantly, until thickened.

Preheat the oven to 350 degrees. Stand the pears in a large casserole and add the water, lemon juice, and sugar. Cover and bake for 45 minutes, then remove from oven and set aside. When ready to serve, place the pears on a serving platter, pour the cooking liquid over them, and top with strawberry sauce.

Nervousness also affected another member of my family – my son Peter when I brought him on for a Father's Day segment more than 25 years ago when he was in his mid-late twenties. Though NBC *Weekend Today in New York* news anchor Felicia Taylor explained to him before we went live that some people get nervous when the "On Air" light goes on, he thought he'd be alright. And he was – until the light actually went on. Peter turned the whitest shade of white we'd ever seen and Felicia signaled her concern to me behind his back. Thinking fast in my position standing right behind him, I grabbed Peter by the back of his belt because I thought he was going to pass out. He ultimately got through it, but it's a story we still laugh about in our house to this day!

A segment we did years ago on Oso Sweet onions from Peru definitely stands out in my memory. The company's logo/mascot was a llama, so the owner sent two live llamas to be part of the segment (I learned that apparently, we needed to have two llamas to be there for each other or they wouldn't stand still) and we brought them up to the studio. Though we never would have been able to stage something like this in these post-9/11 days, back then the segment was a huge hit and we got tremendous press from it.

Years ago, I got caught up in a "controversial" conversation during a segment when I was talking about organic produce, which was growing in popularity around that time. The WNBC news anchor asked me what I thought about organic produce and I offered an economic perspective, explaining that it was currently more expensive because there was less demand for it and subsequently less supply. While I shared that I'm personally more likely to choose organic options when it comes to produce items that grow underground (like root vegetables, etc.), I told the anchor that, "in my own opinion, organic produce isn't worth the price." Sure enough, soon after that, a female viewer tracked me down at my then-house in Bergen County and started banging on my door, screaming "How dare you! *You're killing our children!*" I did my best to calm her down, explaining that my take on organics was only my opinion and assuring her that no farmer – organic or not – wants to kill the people who buy from them!

The produce itself has lent itself to some memorable segments over the years. My friend and anchorwoman Pat Battle is excited to taste everything, although if it's too hot, spicy, or not to her taste, her eyes start to tear up. Pat's also terrified of worms and was always concerned about worms being in corn that I'd bring in from the field; it's been interesting to see each news anchor's produce preferences and concerns over the years. I can understand and sympathize with them because I'm petrified of snakes and am always quick to ask farmers if there are any snakes out in the corn field if we're doing a shoot there. They always laugh and say, "don't worry, they won't hurt you!" Yeah, right….no thanks!

With my WNBC Weekend Today in New York news anchor and friend Pat Battle

Speaking of corn, I was filming in a corn field in Florida for a segment a few years ago that I'll never forget. In this particular segment, we were showing how workers start picking corn on one end of the field in the morning and make their way across the field with a truck following them; they then sort it, box it, and load it onto a truck right then. As I know very well from picking corn as a teen, corn is an incredibly hot, sticky, and exhausting crop to harvest; in addition to the sun beating down on you in the heat of the summer, the leaves of the corn stalks will cut you to shreds if you're not wearing the right protective gear – e.g., long pants and long sleeves – making it doubly hot, manual labor. We did that segment in the Sunshine State in June and there was so much sweat pouring off me that I literally had to change my shirt every five minutes! Every little while I'd take a break and sit in the car with the air conditioning blasting to try to cool off, and even then the photographer kept having to stop because he told me that I was sweating too much!

One of many shirts I changed into during a field segment filmed in a Florida corn field several years ago for NBC 4 New York

That was a tough day, but I felt good about being able to show people what really goes into growing and harvesting different items, and that's always been my goal. Though I love doing segments live in the studio, I think that our taped segments out in the field provide an important public service, helping large parts of the population living in the cities and suburbs better understand where their food comes from and how things are grown and harvested.

CHAPTER 10

OUR FARMERS, OUR FRIENDS

When we started peddling door-to-door in the 1950s, my father established relationships with a lot of farmers. We'd go to the farms themselves or to the Washington Street Market on the Hudson River (which would later evolve into the Hunts Point Market in The Bronx) to buy produce and came to know many of the wholesalers the farmers sold to. On Sunday nights, we traveled to a farmer's market in Newark that attracted farmers from as far away as Vineland and Hammonton in South Jersey, a good two hours' drive each way. We'd often see tomato farmers driving up the New Jersey Turnpike in rack body trucks with their tomatoes in peach baskets stacked 10 rows high. As a kid, I was always amazed at how they'd have hundreds of open baskets on their trucks but would never lose one tomato as they drove. After we opened Napolitano's Produce, farmers started coming direct to us at the store.

We dealt with many farms throughout the state beginning in the 1950s and one of them in south Jersey was Consalo Farms in

Vineland. In the early 2000s, I helped connect the head of Pathmark to the Consalo family and during our conversation, Andy
Consalo and I reminisced about my father; Andy even revealed
to me that they still had my father's phone number (Dumont
5-6765) in their drawer! That surprised me given that nearly 50
years had gone by, but as he explained, "you never know when
you need to call someone!" We were also friendly with Krichmar
Farms, Scapellato Farms, and Marolda Farms in Vineland as
well as with the Diamond Blueberries team in nearby Hammonton. Closer to us in north Jersey, we bought from Sudal Farms
and Francis Johnson's apple farm in Ramsey, DiPiero's Farm in
Montvale, and Demarest Farms in Hillsdale. Wally Smith in New
City, NY was one of the biggest farms we worked with from 1960
onward and Wally initially came to us in a truck with samples of
what he had; every year after that, he'd call on us in the beginning of the season and we'd agree on prices for the whole season.
His and other farmers' produce was picked fresh that day and
our customers would often come to us from 50-60 miles away
to get the corn and tomatoes we carried because they were so
good.

Over the years, people have often asked me the secret to the
incredible taste of our state's tomatoes, corn, peaches, or blueberries and they always look at me in disbelief when I tell them
that there's no magic soil in New Jersey – our produce is just
picked when it's ripe and at its best. If tomatoes are picked in
Florida for export northward, for example, they're picked grass-
green, then transported for days under variable temperature
conditions and just don't taste the same by the time they hit our
markets and are made available to consumers.

For all of those reasons, I learned from an early age that the farmer was our friend. Farmers don't sell manufactured items – there are so many variables and so much hard work, planning, effort, and luck that goes into their yield every season and if they went out, so would we.

Growing up, my father made me and David work at almost every farm we did business with so that we could get a better sense of where the food we sold came from and understand, as he called it, "the value of a package."

For example, one day when I was 13, I remember showing up to Wally Smith's Farm in New City, NY to pick corn wearing a t-shirt and shorts. Wally looked me up and down, laughed, and asked me if I was going to the beach! He promptly gave me a pair of long pants and a jacket, and boy did I need them! I couldn't understand why I had to put them on in 100-degree weather, but I found out soon enough – if you don't, the leaves of the corn stalks will cut you to shreds. Pickers need to walk down many long, tight rows of corn stalks manually inspecting and snapping off each ear, putting them in a sack, and then bundling them in a truck or on a conveyor belt. It's hard labor out there with the sun beating down on you in the heat of the summer; between sweating from the work itself and the presence of dew on the stalks if you're picking first thing in the morning, you end up soaking wet after the day's ears are collected.

Through experiences like that, I learned that farming was a noble profession that required incredibly hard work. Picking corn out in the field is a hot, sticky, manual process, harvesting bananas involves an incredibly labor-intensive, tree-climbing ritual, and beans need to be picked on your hands and knees because they grow on low bushes. Getting products to market is another story – after a 90-day growing process, for example, a box of peppers needs to be harvested, packed, and transported, which requires a whole operational infrastructure, not to mention that not everything that's grown can be sold – for example, only about 20% of a tomato plant's yield might be "perfect" enough to sell.

Given the inherent difficulties of and risk involved in growing fresh produce, it never ceases to amaze me when I hear consumers gripe about having to pay 59 cents for a pound of bananas – they clearly have no idea what goes into growing, harvesting, and transporting that item from the tropics to the convenience of their local store and would never question that relatively low price again if they knew. People will readily pay $5 for a Starbuck's coffee and even $3 for a package of *frozen* vegetables but will complain about having to pay 75 cents for an ear of fresh-picked corn at a local farmer's market. Though fresh produce is incredibly nutritious, great-tasting, and still highly economical pound-for-pound, many people don't perceive the value in it or have seen it even cheaper in weeks, months, or years past and effectively hold it hostage.

The fallout of this consumer bias combined with the increasingly high opportunity cost of property in the New York metro area has been apparent and, over the years, I've watched as farms throughout southern New York and New Jersey have gone out, one by one. Francis Johnson's apple and peach farm became a golf course and then a housing development and Sudal Farms was developed into a townhouse community. As property taxes in north Jersey got higher and higher, it became more lucrative for these farmers to sell their land for other uses, especially if successive generations of their family-owned businesses didn't want to carry on the farming legacy. Most of the farms in our Garden State – once a primarily agricultural society – are now clustered in south and western sections of New Jersey and economic pressures have continued pushing farmers even farther southward into states like Delaware in order to further drive down costs.

Because Napolitano's Produce rode on the success of our suppliers, we always learned to take care of the farmer, and more than 70 years later my message hasn't changed; if anything, it's gotten more urgent in light of all of the current dynamics converging – we need to appreciate, value, and support our local farmers because they feed the nation.

I often think about the gravity of that statement and marvel at what farmers do. For example, 60 billion pounds of potatoes – enough to feed two-thirds of Americans – must be harvested within a six-week window or they'll rot. Potato and all other farmers are up against a range of other challenges as well, from weather conditions and pests to prices, competitors, and more. I feel compelled to talk about the importance of supporting our local farmers practically every week on WNBC.

Years ago, I met Katie and Greg Donaldson and their team at Donaldson's Farm in Hackettstown, NJ after Katie reached out to me on Facebook to thank me for being "the farmer's friend" and speaking out on behalf of the farming industry; we've since become good friends and I've done dozens of remote segments from their location to help educate consumers on how produce is grown and promote awareness of their and other family-owned farms. The same is true of the Kuehm family at Farms View in Wayne, NJ, another long-standing family-owned farm which has graciously allowed me to broadcast dozens of field segments from their site over the years to help shine a light on all of the great and important work they do.

Me and Bette hanging out with Katie Donaldson, co-owner of family-owned Donaldson's Farm in Hackettstown, NJ, during a segment we filmed in their field

With the team at family-owned Farms View in Wayne, NJ

Doing a segment on Jersey corn at Farms View in Wayne, NJ

By no means is this a tale of gloom and doom, however. I see more specialty farms sprouting up all the time and I speak to a growing number of younger farmers getting into the business for the first time because they have a love for it and see its value. So much more farming is computerized these days and, while it may seem at odds with the very definition of farming, this integration of technology and automation enables farmers to be more precise than ever when it comes to planting, irrigating, applying repellants for pests, adding supplemental nutrition, and harvesting, which ultimately helps them optimize their costs and yield. "Vertical farms" (where produce is grown indoors under highly-controlled conditions, often in urban areas that have historically been known as "food deserts" when it comes to fresh produce) as well as rooftop farms are becoming more popular. The same is true of hydroponic operations, which aren't new (they started in Israel, Canada, and Mexico) but have increasingly taken hold because they significantly extend the growing season for produce while removing many of the variables that have traditionally challenged conventional farming. These modern approaches currently focus more on growing leafy items such as lettuces, microgreens, and herbs as well as tomatoes, peppers, and some eggplant varieties as opposed to more intensive crops such as corn, apples, or pineapples and can require a large investment up front, but the value in not having to worry about adverse conditions is high.

I love to see all of this positive activity because more volume keeps prices down for consumers. It's often hard for Americans to understand because they've been schooled to believe that the more they pay for something, the better it is, but that old adage doesn't apply to produce. The laws of supply and demand rule in the produce industry – when prices are cheap, it's because there's an abundance of product, and when there's an abundance of product, it means that the item is in season and should be at its freshest and best-tasting. And that's the time to buy it!

Over the years, I've also found it especially interesting to watch the growth and evolution of the organic produce market. Organic produce used to be hard to sell because it was ugly (since no pesticides were used) and could be 5-6 times the price of conventional produce. Today, organic produce is much prettier and only 2-3 times the price of standard products. While its price points still deter some consumers, those who believe in organics are very loyal and will buy it in a heartbeat.

For years, people have been asking me my opinion on organic produce and whether I think it's worth the price – my answer is that it's up to the individual. Growing up a peddler's son, we didn't think about pesticides or wash anything before we ate it. For myself, I think that opting for organics definitely makes sense for any produce that you're juicing or for "root" items where the part that you eat grows underground. Twenty years ago, I might have hesitated to eat conventional produce that wasn't washed, but today, even standard product uses much less pesticide and relies on more integrative farming methods than ever. Organics are terrific and, though nothing is 100% safe (even "organically-grown" produce may get some non-organic pesticides applied above-ground), conventional produce is pretty safe these days and I would feel fine buying it. So again, it's up to personal preference. One thing I know for sure is that there's no farmer in the world who wants to kill his or her customers!

As someone whose own family business began as a roadside stand, I love farm stands and farmer's markets because there's no middleman – the product is sold directly by farmers in a controlled setting and they're right there to answer any questions a consumer might have. Markets like these bring the consumer much closer to the source of their food, which not only ensures that they'll be getting fresher and more nutritious produce but also helps support farmers and the local economy as well as build a sense of community.

In today's competitive market, farmers often leave the industry not for selfish reasons but because they can't keep up with the demands of the job as they age and none of their offspring want to follow in their footsteps; most who stay in the business are able to because they have kids who want to take it over. There are a lot of opportunities in farming for the right candidate and I've always thought, what's better than working outside (or inside) growing things that feed and sustain people? I can't think of anything more important or virtuous than that.

I hope that people will appreciate farms and farmers because they're a precious resource that's becoming increasingly rare; you never see houses being knocked down to build a farm, if you know what I mean. We need to support our local farmers and farmer's markets because when they're gone, they're gone forever and there's no going back.

CHAPTER 11

THE APPEAL OF PRODUCE PETE

Following, Pete's colleagues, friends, and family members share their favorite anecdotes about Pete and why they think he's had such longevity on TV:

Tere Mele, Stage Manager, WNBC Weekend Today in New York

"I've known Pete since around 1998. He started doing segments at WNBC before I started, but as soon as I began working on the weekend show as the stage manager, he and I became instant friends. He was funny, generous, sweet, and honest and to this day, he's never changed.

We all became a family on the show. Pete and Bette would have parties and invite the whole gang from WNBC; they still throw a holiday party and make sure that we're all available before they set the date in December.

Throughout the year, we're all always invited to his relatives' parties too – whether it's his kids, grandkids, or siblings. Pete and I have this thing where we say I'm his 'work wife,' though I think he also says that about Pat Battle, so we share him! When we were in the studio, he'd give me a ride home after the show on Saturday or drop me off wherever I needed to go and jokingly say that if he's not there, he'll send a car for me….but I know that deep down, if I ever needed anything, Pete would be there. He's always had such a kind heart and we all know everything about each other; he's that way with his friends and family members as well. He's always been the same person and never tries to be someone else – he truly is Produce Pete, a loveable, kind, sweet, funny, big teddy bear. If his family members or friends are sad, he's sad. All while I was "furloughed" during the pandemic, he constantly called or emailed me to see how I was doing and if I needed anything.

As far as what we do, Pete does a "tease" for what he'll be talking about in his weekly segment. He says something like, "today we're going to talk about Jersey tomatoes... and here's my little tomato" (meaning *me*), and I waltz in, we're on camera for about 10 seconds, then we laugh and go to a commercial break. One day he said, "and here comes my mother!!!!!" It was just one of those days and it didn't bother me, but we all got texts and

117

emails about it. It was all in good fun and we laughed about it for a week until the next show.

Pete is himself and what you see is what you get. His family didn't have money growing up; he started peddling produce at an early age, never had anything handed to him, and always worked, which made him the person he is today. He still works his butt off. He'll always be the way he is. That's why people have loved him and why he's lasted so long on TV – we're family!"

Pat Battle, Co-Anchor, NBC 4 New York Weekend Today in New York

"I first met Pete when I joined WNBC *Weekend Today in New York* as a co-anchor around 2004. Before that, I'd seen him on the air on *People Are Talking* and knew who he was, but we'd never met. After meeting him, it didn't matter what fruit or vegetable he was talking about, I was sold on Pete. He's just larger than life and so warm. Underneath his colorful antics, he's a peddler's son and just such a humble guy who can't believe the success he's achieved, for which he's so grateful. He's extremely good at what he does, always researches his topics, and tells beautiful stories; beyond his honesty, humility, and genuine love of family, he's just a regular guy who's made it to a place he never imagined and never takes it for granted. He's so happy to share what he knows and what he feels with a larger audience. It's all about food and family and those memorable experiences.

Pete and I are the product of completely different life experiences, but we have a surprising amount in common. Though my parents are from the deep south and his were immigrants from Italy and Ireland, our parents rose to great heights from humble beginnings. Pete and I are very different people, but outside of the show, we talk at least once a week and I know and love Bette and his whole family.

Pete and I have had so many funny moments on the show over the years. I'll never forget one time about 10 years ago when Pete brought in blackberries for his segment. I said to him on the air, "You know what they say about blackberries, right? The blacker the berry, the sweeter the juice!" – a saying which

came from the African American community. Pete just gave me a shocked look, said "Oh, Patricia!" and turned beet red! It was funny, and now that's our thing every year when he brings in blackberries – he always asks me if I'm going to say that again. We have that kind of relationship; we let each other be who we are, are very respectful of each other, and work well together. We have a very natural flow because we're genuinely friends. And we like to make jokes during commercial breaks, which is why we're often laughing when we come back on air!

Another thing about Pete is that he has a heart of gold. During the pandemic, I was doing a story about a church in Hackensack, NJ that was handing out food to those in need but unfortunately ran out, leaving long lines of hungry people unaddressed. I felt so bad and immediately picked up the phone and called Pete at S. Katzman Produce at the Hunts Point Market; Pete and Steve Katzman immediately sent a truckload of fresh fruit and vegetables – some 17,000 pounds of food! – to support the cause and continued to send a truckload of food to that church every week, feeding thousands of families for months. I always know where Pete's heart is. I didn't hesitate to call him and I knew he'd know just what to do; he knows what it's like to not have essentials and would always want to help. He's just a good man.

I think that the secret to Pete's longevity on TV is that he's just like us. He's a regular guy who pops up on your TV every weekend, tells real-life stories, and tries to get you to eat right so you can live right. His life hasn't been easy, like any of ours, and he's never aspired to do anything different – he loves what he does and is very happy telling viewers about asparagus and broccoli rabe every week. I'm grateful for our friendship and for the positive effect he's had on me – I wasn't big on Brussels sprouts, asparagus, and certain other fruits and vegetables before I met him, but I am now!"

Gus Rosendale, Co-Anchor, NBC 4 New York Weekend Today in New York

"Our family on Long Island grew up watching WNBC, so I've known Pete's work since his beginnings at Channel 4 in New York and I've personally worked with him since 2012. Television is a tough and sometimes fickle business, but an audience detects and usually appreciates someone who's 'the real deal,' and that's Pete. The Pete you see on TV is the same one you meet in person.

Pete's passion for and knowledge of his subject are obvious, but I also think it's apparent that he's a kind person. I think people like waking up to that in the morning.

The first time I was going to do a segment with Pete, I actually spent time researching the topic so that I'd have something akin to perceptive questions about potatoes or whatever the heck was being featured on the broadcast. Pat Battle just laughed when I told her that. As I've learned, the anchor's job is to let

Pete be Pete and just gently keep the segment running on time. It works, and we usually stay on time. Usually.

A lot of the newscast involves tough subjects; that's the nature of news. Pete's couple of minutes on the program are a break from the mayhem, reminding us that we still need to cook and gather around the table for a good meal. We all need that perspective."

Raphael Miranda, NBC 4 New York Meteorologist

"I've been working the weekend shift since I arrived at WNBC 4 New York, and that's Pete's shift too, so I've had the pleasure of working with Pete for over 10 years now. Saturdays are extra-special because of him – and not just because I get to take home the produce and whatever yummy thing Bette has whipped up.

To know Pete is to love him, and I can say the same of his family. I know this because Pete is a giver and it's in his nature to share. He shares his food, his passion, his family, his home, and his stories. He's one of the few people in my life where if I ever needed to knock on someone's door at 2 a.m. for any reason, he'd be the one to help, no questions asked. Pete and his family invited me, my husband, and son Mac to Mac's first baseball game (we saw the Somerset Patriots play in New Jersey) and it was a day we'll never forget; the game was great and the weather was perfect.

Pete was in his element, throwing out the first pitch, talking to his throngs of fans about produce, and at one point even tossing ears of corn (or maybe it was tomatoes?) to them!

The secret to Pete's success and longevity on TV is simple – fans love Pete because he's real. He's a mensch and it shows. Pete and Bette have the whole station over for a holiday lunch every year. They put out an incredible buffet and we all get to enjoy how they celebrate the holidays – Bette's broccoli salad and eggplant parmigiana/rollatini are legendary, there are pictures of Santa on the walls, and the house is decorated in Christmas fabulousness inside and out. To be honest, it's one of the highlights of the holidays for me and my family.

The way Pete invites you to become part of his family during the holidays is just an example of why we love him. And of course, when it comes to produce, there IS no other source."

Mama Louise's (and Bette's) Best Broccoli Salad

Yields 6-8 servings

2 heads broccoli, cut into small pieces

½ cup golden raisins

½ small onion, red or white diced

½ pound bacon, cooked and crumbled

1 cup cashew nuts

Dressing

1½ cups mayonnaise

3-4 tablespoons red wine or balsamic vinegar

1/3 cup sugar

In a large bowl, mix together all of the salad ingredients. In a small bowl, whisk together the dressing ingredients, then stir into the salad until well coated with dressing. Chill and serve.

Katie Donaldson, Co-Owner of family-owned Donaldson Farms & Farm Market, Hackettstown, NJ

"Years ago, on a Saturday morning, I heard someone say, "You've *got* to support your local farmers. Do you know how hard it is to grow and pick this asparagus?! And boy, is it delicious!"

I switched my focus to the TV and there, on WNBC 4 New York, was Produce Pete. The timing couldn't have been better, because at that same moment I was posting a photo that I had just taken of our farm staff harvesting asparagus! Pete's sentiments about the labor of love in farm work were just what I was planning to convey in my post. I quickly found his Facebook page and shared our photo along with a heartfelt 'Thank You' for supporting local farmers.

I grew up partly in New Milford, next to Bergenfield where Napolitano's Produce was a staple in the neighborhood for nearly 50 years. I feel a connection to the areas of Jersey that don't easily get to experience a modern working produce farm. So many families benefit from learning about where their food comes from and the hard work behind it. I was impressed that Pete was the voice sharing that message.

Shortly after our social media connection, Pete and his lovely wife Bette surprised me with a visit to the farm and our Donaldson Farms family made quick friends. Pete is one of the most hard-working guys we know. He understands the ever-changing produce scene in the tri-state area and gladly shares his experiences to help others evolve and grow. We like to refer to him as 'the greatest ambassador of local agriculture and family business.'

Pete and Bette are a dynamic duo; his home-grown knowledge of produce and the ins and outs of family businesses combined with her decorating skills and incredible knack for creating mouth-watering dishes for every season make them quite a team! They take great pride in their family and are clearly cherished by their children and grandchildren. Pete weaves his wisdom into relevant, timeless stories and anecdotes that educate, entertain, and remind you that at the heart of everything is family."

Tom Santomarco, Producer, NBC 4 New York Weekend Today in New York

"I've known Pete personally for several years through the show, but I've known who he was from TV since I was a little kid. It's surreal to now have a personal and professional relationship with Pete after growing up in New York City knowing him from his segments.

People need to know that Pete is in real life who he is on TV. He's a very genuine person – what you see is what you get – and I mean that in the best possible way. He and his wife Bette treat the WNBC team like family.

The secret to Pete's success and longevity on TV is his authenticity. He's folksy but very smart. No one knows produce as well as him, and certainly no one can talk about it as clearly or informatively. It's also the way he ties fruits and vegetables back to his family history; there's always a memory to share and they're very relatable."

Maddie (Rosemary) Henri, TV Programming & Development Executive

"I was Executive Producer of the show *People Are Talking*, which premiered on WWOR-TV in the metro New York market in 1987. At the top of each show, we'd cover a big news story from the newspapers and on one particular winter day in late 1988/early 1989 there was a big scare over grapes from South America and whether they were safe to eat, so we decided to cover it. I asked my associate producer Renee to "find a grocer who can talk about whether we can eat these grapes or not." She went through the phone book, found Napolitano's Produce in Bergenfield, NJ, and called his store. Ten minutes later she informed me, "he doesn't want to come; he's busy." I said, "what do you *mean* he doesn't want to come?" I thought he'd be a real expert whom people could trust and I couldn't understand why he wouldn't want to come on TV for two minutes and just talk about his expertise as a grocer. Renee called him several more times after that, but still had no luck. I finally said to her, "call him back and offer him a limo," but even that didn't impress or sway Pete! Finally, his wife Bette decided that "he'll do it!" and the car was sent.

Pete brought grapes with him for the live segment and as he talked about them, he also ate a few grapes to show that they were safe. I thought he was so raw and real – a diamond in the rough. I called my boss, Bob Woodruff, who was head of programming, and said, "are you watching this? Don't you think he'd make a great regular segment? I'll work with him and, without changing who he is, I know I can make him really good." Bob said, "I love that idea." After the segment I told Pete, "you're a little rough, but you're real. If I work with you, would you like to do weekly segments on the show?" He said yes. Pete knows his business well and is so natural that I knew a teleprompter would kill his charm. I told him just to talk about what he knows – hold the fruit or vegetable in your hands, show it, talk about it in terms of when to buy it, how to pick it using your five senses, etc. – and he just got better and better. I eventually suggested that he add a recipe, so Bette would make a dish for each featured fruit or vegetable. We started offering the recipes, which became very popular.

On our show, Pete was called 'Pete Your Produce Pal' and he had shirts and aprons made. His name was perfect – it was all about helping viewers. I eventually left that show and went on to jobs at Lifetime, Universal, and HGTV and Pete went on to do a daytime show called *House Party* with Steve Doocy, but he and I stayed in touch and he always shared his latest opportunities with me, which was fabulous.

My parents, like Pete's, were Italian immigrants and his family reminded me so much of my own – from their work ethic to our big Sunday family dinners. Pete came from humble roots and people like him are the backbone of our society. I remember that my dad always used to say to us, "only in America," and Pete is the perfect reflection of that; he's always remained so humbled by and grateful for his success, which is the beauty of it all.

When my daughter was getting married and needed tiny clementines with stems for her décor, the florist was going to charge a ridiculous price to get them, so I called Pete for help. He ordered them for me and met me with cases of them in his car. That's Pete – he'd do anything for you.

Pete's authenticity has never changed. Viewers related to the family, work, and life stories he shared during his segments. I often told him to always be himself. On TV, people either connect to you or they don't. You need to be authentic and truthful, and that's his secret – he's always Pete."

Judy Libonati, co-owner of Libonati's Tavern in Bergenfield, NJ

"Beginning in 1969, my husband Rich and I owned Libonati's Tavern in Bergenfield, the restaurant next door to the store owned by Pete's father (and later Pete). Pete's father knew Rich's father, Gerald, and eventually sold Rich the building Napolitano's Produce was located in; we then rented Pete's space back to him when he took over his family business in 1970.

Pete's a warm, good-hearted person and he's also really funny – we used to laugh all the time. He was always very personable and his store was well-known in the area because it had been there so long. Pete relates to the average person and talks to people in a language they understand. I used to laugh every time I'd see him on TV because it's fun to see someone you know on television. Bette is also so loving and their family is so important to them.

We sold the tavern in 2002 and moved to Phoenix but always had great memories of our friendship with Pete and Bette and the many special times Pete and Rich spent together, whether working at side-by-side businesses for decades (and commiserating about how hard their jobs were!), golfing, or socializing. We consider them family."

Dana Kuehm, co-owner of family-owned Farms View Farm Market & Garden Center in Wayne, NJ

"When I was a kid in the 1970s, we didn't grow our own corn at our farm; we used to buy it from a farmer named Wally Smith in New City, NY. I remember that they'd put the corn on the back of our truck and we would unload it when we got back. On more than one occasion, I remember seeing Pete at Wally's farm picking up corn for his store, though I didn't know him then. Later, Pete became a customer of ours and as we reminisced, we realized we'd met previously – we'd both known and had bought corn from Wally Smith.

Since then, Pete has filmed dozens of segments at our farm over the years and he attended my father's funeral in 2016. A few years ago, I fondly remember my sons Alec and Adam having a great time driving Pete around our field on a quad so that he didn't have to walk all the way out to our tomato and pumpkin patches in the hot sun. The greatest thing about him is that he's so natural and never feels the need to redo his segments over and over – he wants to come across exactly as he is.

Pete is an honest, real, and sincere person and I think that's the secret to his success. When people see him at our farm and ask him questions or want to take a picture with him – which happens all the time – he's so friendly and approachable and is always happy to oblige them and tell them a story or a joke. We appreciate Pete and all he's done for farms like ours throughout the state and we treasure his friendship and support....and we now have Pete convinced that fresh-picked corn should only be cooked for three minutes, not four!"

Stephen Katzman, Owner & President of S. Katzman Produce, The Bronx, NY

"Growing up in Teaneck, I knew Pete and his family's roadside stand. The Napolitanos were customers of ours at Hunts Point Market and I remember loading Pete's father's truck when I was 13; during my summers in college, I used to work at our family business and saw Pete then too, because he used to buy a majority of his produce from us and a few other suppliers. Pete was a nice guy who worked his ass off and had a tough father. When his father turned the business over to him in 1969/1970, he told all of us suppliers at Hunt's Point not to call him if Pete didn't pay and my father stepped in to vouch for Pete. Pete has always said that he wouldn't have made it in the business if it weren't for my father standing up for his character and reputation, but I don't believe that's true. I think that Pete would always have made it because he worked hard and was a hustler; he always looked for value in the package and knew he could sell it.

Pete used to come pick up produce from us at 2-3 a.m. in an old, beat-up blue truck. We had a busy market where there wasn't enough parking for all of the trucks that would come, especially around the holidays, and I'll never forget one time when Pete was in his 20s, he backed his truck in to pick up his stuff and another truck double-parked him. Pete was in a rush to get back to his own store to set up for their opening that morning and ended up getting into a fist fight with the guy in our parking lot!

One thing about Pete is that the produce he carried had to be the best and eat great. Anything you bought out of Pete's store was the best. When he was in the business, it was top-notch and he was the only one I'd buy from for any baskets I sent as gifts. Pete's always been one of the most honest people I know and his family comes first; I've always liked my kids to spend time with him to hear his stories and be exposed to him. He's also a lot of fun to be around; he's got a great personality and will do anything for a friend. If you're lucky enough to be a friend of his, you're a friend for life.

We'd sell flowers at our store every spring and I'll never forget one time when a grower of ours in Pennsylvania gave me some 'Sweet William' flowers. Pete was one of our customers and knew that if I didn't sell the flowers, my father wouldn't let me go home, so he bought 20 boxes from me. Bette later told me that Pete threw them in the garbage as soon as he got home! We still joke about it, but I'll never forget what he did for me to help me meet my 'quota' and keep me in good standing with my father.

I think Pete's long-time success on TV comes from the fact that it's never been about the money for him. He enjoys what he does and has never been full of himself; he's very humble and straight-forward. He treats everyone with respect until they give him reason not to. He's worked with us at our company for the last

20 years and he understands that it's my grandfather's name up there and that we never want to tarnish that. With every load of product that comes in, there's paperwork, pricing terms, and quality reports that need to be completed or reviewed for accuracy. I have Pete look at them, then I look at them and sign the check; he's extremely detail-oriented and the only one I trust to help cover that important function for us. It's unusual to find people of Pete's caliber and I consider myself lucky. He calms down my toughest customers and is really invaluable, both as a colleague and a friend. We're truly family."

Bob Welch, Pete's best friend since 1950

"I grew up in Englewood and Pete and I met in kindergarten. Though he eventually moved and we ended up going to different schools after that year, we remained best friends and worked together all our lives, first at my uncle's liquor store in the 1960s and then at Pete's store, where I worked doing

anything and everything until the 1990s. Pete is a wonderful person whom I love very much and we got along great, whether it was working, fishing, golfing, or spending time together with our families.

I was a firefighter in the City of Englewood until my retirement and I'll never forget one time when Pete quit working for his father at the store for a year or so – he began working as a plumber and accidentally set a house on fire in Englewood when he went into a wall with a torch. My crew and I responded to the scene and put out the fire, but it wasn't long after that that Pete gave up his plumbing career and went back to the store!

Pete is very funny and personable, has classic stories, and people love him. I think his success on TV stems from the fact that he knows his produce and is a real person, like your next-door neighbor."

Alexandra Hartman, Pete's granddaughter

"Growing up, people always recognized our Poppy on the street, especially when we tagged along at book signings or appearances. It was weird in the beginning, but now I admire it and feel proud when people tell him how much they love watching him or how he changed their life. He's a very caring and loving grandfather and sees that people look up to him, so he's very respectful of people and fans.

He's very hard-working and has told us a lot of stories about his childhood. Every summer, our whole family goes down to the Jersey shore for a vacation and I look forward to it every year, especially when he cooks for us because he makes the best steaks ever. I remember being at the store when he still owned it and it was very busy.

It makes me proud to see him on TV because he's worked so hard to be there, and my friends all watch him too. I think he resonates with people because he's a very warm person who helps them learn new things; people feel like they know him and that he's a friend. I love all of his colleagues at WNBC and remember going on *Weekend Today in New York* with him for a segment when I was about eight years old; he's brought all of his seven grandkids on the show with him to cover different produce items over the years. It's kind of cool how he's talked about all of us and our accomplishments on TV!

It's great to have Produce Pete as our grandfather and I hope that he stays on TV because he loves what he does."

CHAPTER 12

PETE'S PICKS

After being in the produce industry for so long, you get to learn the easiest and best ways to select, store, and prepare everything from apples to zucchinis. Here are some of my favorite tips and fun facts concerning some of the most popular produce items:

- *Artichokes* – However you prepare your artichokes (raw, fried, creamed, marinated, stuffed, etc.), be sure to avoid cooking them in an aluminum pot because it will turn them a gray-green color. To prepare them for the pot, rinse the artichokes in cold water, handling them carefully so that you don't prick yourself on their pointed barbs. While the barbs are softer and easier to handle after the artichoke is cooked, many people opt to remove them beforehand by snipping off the tips of the leaves with kitchen shears or scissors.

Growing up, my family always loved artichokes and there wasn't a holiday where artichokes weren't on our table, especially Thanksgiving. Bette has proudly carried on the tradition of my mom's recipe. Even my late golden retriever, Montana, would sit in the kitchen while Bette was making stuffed artichokes and bark until she gave him some!

Bette's Super-Delicious Stuffed Artichokes

(makes 4 stuffed artichokes)

- 4 medium-sized artichokes
- 2 cups breadcrumbs
- ¼ cup Parmesan cheese
- 1 tablespoon garlic powder
- ½ teaspoon freshly ground black pepper
- ½ cup (1 stick) butter, melted
- ¼ cup water
- ¾ cup olive oil
- 2 tablespoons parsley flakes

Rinse each artichoke well, then remove the small outer leaves from the bottom row around the artichoke, cut off the stem, and slice about one inch off the top. In a large bowl, combine the breadcrumbs, Parmesan cheese, garlic powder, and pepper. Add the melted butter, water, and oil and mix well, adding more water or oil if necessary to make the stuffing very moist. Turn the artichokes upside down and press firmly to spread the leaves, then turn right side up and stand the artichokes in a large pot with about 1½ inches of water in the bottom. Cover and steam over medium-high heat for about 20-25 minutes or until the artichokes are tender, checking the water level occasionally and adding more water as needed. Stuff the breadcrumb mixture into the center and inside surrounding layers of leaves. Put into a pan, cover tightly with foil, and place in a 350-degree oven for approximately 20 minutes (or else put onto a microwavable plate and microwave for approximately 3-4 minutes) and enjoy!

- **Asparagus** – Steam or braise asparagus spears in a small amount of water, but don't overcook them or they'll turn into a tasteless mush. Asparagus tips tend to cook faster than the stem ends, so try standing them up in a narrow pot and steaming them in about an inch of water. I fondly remember my Irish grandmother cooking asparagus in a coffee pot – she'd tie the bunch of spears around with string, stand them in an inch or two of water, and cook them for about five minutes, or until tender but still crisp. You can also sauté asparagus for three or four minutes with butter, adding a spoonful of water as necessary to prevent burning.

- **Avocados** – Leave firm avocados out on the counter for a few days to ripen them, but if you want to hasten that process, put the avocados in a paper bag or a drawer; some people think they ripen best wrapped in foil. Avocado flesh exposed to the air will darken very quickly; some people think that leaving the pit in prevents discoloration, but the primary factor in preventing discoloration is keeping air away from the flesh, so wrap a cut avocado in plastic, refrigerate, and use it as soon as possible. Peeled and sliced avocados should be sprinkled with lemon or lime juice to retard discoloration, and the citric acid will also bring out the flavor. To professionally peel an avocado, cut it lengthwise around the pit, then rotate the two halves in opposite directions to open the fruit cleanly. Gently put the tip of a spoon under the pit; if it comes out easily, the avocado is ripe.

- **Bananas** – Bananas should actually be peeled from the bottom, not the top, because peeling from the bottom ensures no strings; if you watch monkeys, the ultimate banana experts, they always peel bananas from the bottom. If you wrap the top part of the banana near the stalk with plastic wrap, it will slow the ripening process. Another fun fact – the peel of a banana can also be used to give your shoes a great shine!

- **Citrus Fruit** – Fans have heard me say this for years and it will probably end up on my epitaph when I go – when selecting oranges or grapefruits at the store, choose fruits that feel "heavy in the hand" for their size. This will indicate that their interior flesh is juicy and fresh.

- **Corn** – It's best to eat fresh corn right away; otherwise, store it in the refrigerator. Also, never strip corn until you're ready to cook it, a mistake many people make. I often see people in supermarkets stripping the husks from corn so that they don't have to deal with the mess at home, but all they're doing is letting heat into the corn, which accelerates its conversion from sugar to starch. The husk of the corn was designed by Mother Nature to protect the corn and keep it fresh, so keep it intact until you're ready to eat it. Here's some simple recipes from my friend and farmer Wally Smith, who delivered fresh corn to our store every morning for over 30 years.

  ➤ **Best Boiled Corn** – Bring a pot of water to a boil before dropping in the shucked ears. If the ears are too long for the pot, don't cut them with a knife, which tends to crush the kernels – just break them in two with your hands. Let the water return to a boil, and boil hard for 3-4 minutes. Remove immediately and serve; don't let the corn stand in the water.

  ➤ **Great Grilled Corn** – Pull down the husks but don't detach them and remove the silks. Spread butter and salt on the kernels if you wish, then pull the husks back up and twist closed. Grill the ears for about fifteen minutes, turning often.

  ➤ **Easy Microwaved Corn** – Shuck corn, spread with butter if you wish, cover closely with plastic wrap or waxed paper, and microwave on full power (100 percent) for about 2½ minutes per ear.

- **Deterring Fruit Flies** – If you find that fruit left out on your counter to ripen during warm-weather months attracts pesky fruit flies, try this trick – pour red wine vinegar into a cup and leave it out on the counter near your fruit. The sweetness of the liquid will attract the fruit flies and they'll eventually fall/drown in the cup.

- **Mangoes** – people always ask me how to cut and eat a mango, so here are the results of my years of experience. To deal with the pit in the center, take two lengthwise cuts on either side of where you think the pit is; if it's a flattish mango, turn it up so a narrow side is facing you. The pit is large but fairly flat, so make the cuts no more than half an inch on either side of an imaginary center line. You'll have three slices, the center one with the pit in it. Now take the two outside slices and score the flesh with the tip of a knife, getting as close to the skin as you can without breaking it. Hold the scored slice in two hands and gently push up from the skin side, which will pop inside out. The segments of mango will separate and can easily be scooped off the skin with a spoon or butter knife. Add a sprinkle of lime juice if you like.

- **Pineapples** – Though many people think that a pineapple is ripe if they can easily pull a leaf out of the crown, in actuality this test doesn't tell you anything useful. Like tomatoes, pineapples are considered mature when they develop a little color break; if it's begun to turn a little orange or red, you'll be able to ripen it at home. To ripen a pineapple, stand it upside down on its leaf end on the counter – which helps the sugar flow towards the top and keeps the pineapple from fermenting at the bottom – and let it ripen for a few days.

- **Strawberries** – Strawberries are an exception to my no-refrigeration rule – they must be refrigerated. To prevent their breakdown, only wash them when you're ready to eat them.

- **Tomatoes** – Among the most important rules to remember about tomatoes is to avoid putting them on the windowsill or in the sun to ripen. Just put them out on the counter, stem end up, in a relatively cool place – not right next to the stove or the dishwasher. Also, never, ever refrigerate tomatoes, not even after the tomato is ripe. Refrigerating them kills their flavor, nutrients, and texture – it just kills the tomato, period. If you've got too many ripe tomatoes, make a salad or a raw tomato sauce for pasta, or make a cooked sauce and freeze it for another time.

Bette's Best Jersey Fresh Tomato Sauce

(makes 8-10 servings)

5 pounds Jersey tomatoes

¼ cup olive oil

2 teaspoons fresh garlic, chopped

1 teaspoon salt

1 teaspoon freshly ground black pepper

½ cup sugar

2 teaspoons fresh or dried oregano

2 tablespoons chopped fresh Italian parsley or dried parsley

1 teaspoon fresh or dried basil

Rinse the tomatoes well, cut out the cores, and cut the tomatoes in half. Place the tomatoes in a blender and purée until smooth. In a large saucepan, heat the oil over moderate heat. Add the garlic and brown for 1 minute; then add the tomatoes. Add the remaining ingredients and cover the pan. Simmer for 1 hour, stirring occasionally. Serve over your favorite cooked pasta or freeze in containers for later use.

While we're at it, here are some of my musings on life as well – some simple things I learned along the way that may help you enhance your happiness, health, and longevity:

- **On Marriage** – You have to be friends with your partner first and foremost. Bette and I got married young and we've had plenty of fights along the way; we even went to a marriage counselor years ago. But she's always been there for me and I can't picture my life without her. Relationships are all about commitment and compromise.

Bette and I on our wedding day in 1967 at a tree in Bergenfield, NJ where we posed for pictures….and more recently recreating the scene at that very same tree for our 50th anniversary in 2017. We've now been married for 55 years and are still going strong!

- **On Children** – I think that I was a good provider because my kids had everything they needed, but I wasn't great about going to their games, taking them to the park, etc.;

I said that it was because I was always working. The fact is, they were raised by a fantastic mother (Bette). I learned that you need to be a great parent every day and I regret putting work ahead of them all the time. I've tried to make up for it by being a good Poppy to my grandkids today. If I could do everything over again, I think that you can be successful in your professional life while still giving your kids some quality time.

- **On Work** – Though I came to hate running the store day in and day out, I had a family to support and I liked stability, so I brought a good work ethic to it. I applied that same work ethic to my segments on TV, which is a job I really enjoy. I get to the studio early, ask questions, and encourage colleagues and fans to share feedback and constructive criticism because I see it as helpful. In the end, there's no free ride and you have to work hard at anything to succeed at it, but I feel that there's tremendous honor in that.

- **On Time** – Though I'm in my late seventies now, I feel like I'm 20. When you look back on it, life goes by so quickly, so don't take life or your family for granted.

- **On Relationships** – Don't let things go unsaid, good or bad, for years – holding in anger or resentment eats away at you, makes you sick, and ages you. Though it can be hard sometimes, try not to sweat the small stuff or let foolish things aggravate you. Be kind to people and realize that most of them are trying to be good and do the right thing.

- **Things My Father Taught Me** – Not a day goes by that I'm not reminded of something my father used to say; while his insights used to drive me crazy as a kid, it's amazing how simple, honest, and true his advice turned out to be. Some of his favorite sayings included:

  ➢ "Always treat your customers like family; without them, you have nothing"

  ➢ "It's easier to tell the truth than a lie" (he also warned that "a lie stays with you forever")

  ➢ "Success comes from hard work, nothing else"

  ➢ "12 midnight is only a time – it doesn't mean it's time to quit work" (I especially hated that one as a kid!)

  ➢ "Family is everything"

  ➢ "You can't make people like you, so don't worry about what other people think of you"

  ➢ "It's better to try and fail than to not try at all"

  ➢ "If you work hard, you make your own luck"

  ➢ "Don't ever forget where you came from"

  ➢ "We're only here for a short time, so make the most of it"

  ➢ "Camminare intorno all'isolato" (this Italian saying translates to 'walk around the block' – in other words, don't react to a situation immediately, say something you'll regret, and burn bridges; rather, take a moment to cool down and think things through. I've taught this important lesson to my kids and grandkids as well)

➢ "You may not think so now, but your humble beginnings will turn out to be your best asset"

- **On Health** – We didn't have a lot growing up and, being in the produce business, we ate what was seasonal and on the truck – a lot of greens, fruits, and vegetables. It turned out that our default diet back then is the basis of a healthy foundation for anyone. As I've always said – and it doesn't get much simpler than this – "if you eat right, you're gonna live right!"

A promotional shot for NBC 4 New York featuring my mantra

CHAPTER 13

GET COOKING!
MORE FAVORITE FAMILY RECIPES

Between my mother, my wife Bette, and our many relatives and family friends, I've been surrounded by great cooks and stand-out dishes my whole life. Following are just some of the signature recipes – all containing a fresh fruit or vegetable as the star player – that have etched a place in my heart and memory bank over the years. They're simple, sensational, and I know you'll love them too!

Bette's Vidalia Sweet Onion Pie

It can be hard to figure out what to do with onions and I didn't think I would like this recipe when Bette first made it, but this pie is one of my favorites and you can use any kind of sweet onion if Vidalias aren't available. Even if you don't like onions, you're going to love this recipe!

1½ cups buttery crackers, finely crushed

6 tablespoons (¾ stick) unsalted butter, room temperature

2 cups Vidalia onions, thinly sliced

¾ cup whole milk

5 eggs

¾ teaspoon salt

¾ cup packed grated sharp cheddar cheese

Paprika

Chopped fresh parsley

Preheat oven to 350° F. Mix crackers and 4 tablespoons butter in bowl until well blended. Press mixture on bottom and one inch up the sides of an 8-inch pie plate. Melt remaining 2 tablespoons butter in heavy medium skillet over medium heat. Add onions and sauté until tender, about 12 minutes. Arrange onions in cracker crust. Beat milk, eggs, and salt in medium bowl until blended. Season with pepper. Pour egg mixture over onions in crust, sprinkle cheese over filling, and sprinkle with paprika. Bake pie until knife inserted into center comes out clean, about 35 minutes. Garnish with parsley and serve.

Eggplant Rollatini

We throw a Christmas party for my "NBC family" every year and Bette's eggplant rollatini is always a huge hit. It's a hearty dish and the use of tangy and nutritious eggplant is a great swap for pasta.

2 eggplants, cut lengthwise into 1/8-inch or ¼-inch slices

2 eggs, beaten

¼ cup milk

Bread crumbs

Salt to taste

Vegetable or olive oil

Prepared tomato sauce

Filling

2 pounds ricotta cheese

1 pound mozzarella cheese, shredded

1 cup Parmesan or Romano cheese grated

2 eggs

1 tablespoon garlic powder

Preheat oven to 350° F. Dip eggplant slices in egg and milk mixture, then coat both sides with bread crumbs. In a large frying pan, heat oil over medium-high heat until hot and fry eggplant slices until golden brown; drain on paper towels and set aside. In a large bowl, mix together all of the filling ingredients. In a large baking pan, place sauce on bottom of pan to cover. Spread a thin layer of cheese mixture onto each slice of eggplant, roll up tightly, and place seam side down in baking pan. Once the pan is filled with the rollatini, pour sauce over the rolls, top with shredded mozzarella cheese, and sprinkle some Parmesan or Romano cheese over top. Bake for 20-25 minutes until cheese is melted and lightly browned.

Broccoli Rabe & Sausage

Ever since I was a little boy, this dish has been on our table a least once a week. The recipe never changed (except when my family didn't have money for sausage, and then my mother would use whatever leftovers we had; mostly chicken, though whatever she added always tasted good). Mom taught Bette how to make it and I still love it; even my kids and grandchildren love it. I guess it's in the genes!

2 pounds broccoli rabe (approximately 2 bunches)

¼ cup olive oil

3 cloves garlic, peeled and sliced

1 pound sausage, hot or sweet

½ teaspoon hot red crushed pepper

Salt and pepper to taste

Cooked pasta (optional)

In a large frying pan, brown sausage. After sausage is cooked, cut into approximately ¼-inch circular pieces and set aside. Cut off about 2 inches from the bottom stem of the broccoli rabe; rinse well and drain. In a large pot, put in broccoli rabe and add approximately 4 cups of water; cover and steam on medium-high until tender, stirring occasionally. In colander, drain broccoli rabe and set aside. In the same empty pot, add oil and garlic and sauté garlic until lightly browned. Add broccoli rabe, sausage, crushed red pepper, salt, and pepper to the sautéed garlic and oil and stir together. If desired, place broccoli rabe over cooked pasta and serve.

Bette's Best Marinated Zucchini

This marinated zucchini recipe is easy and a real winner, especially at the holidays. What makes it especially unique is the incorporation of mint, which gives it a completely different and memorable taste!

4 zucchini

¼ cup olive oil

¼ cup balsamic vinegar

½ teaspoon mint leaves, fresh or dried

3 cloves garlic, chopped

Salt and pepper to taste

Slice zucchini with skins on. In a large skillet, heat oil and fry until golden brown. Set aside. In a medium casserole, layer the fried zucchini with vinegar, chopped garlic, salt, pepper, and mint leaves. Cover casserole and let zucchini marinate at room temperature. You can serve it hot or at room temperature.

Zucchini Bread

In addition to being a delicious and healthy dessert, zucchini bread is a great way to sneak vegetables into your kids' diet. Bette's been making this recipe in our house for years, first for our kids when they were young and now for my seven grandchildren, and they all love it. Trying to get kids to eat zucchini can be a task, but they really enjoy it when it's presented in the form of zucchini bread.

Yields 8-10 servings

3 cups flour

2 cups sugar (or less to taste)

1 teaspoon salt

1 teaspoon ground cinnamon

½ teaspoon baking soda

3 eggs

1 cup corn or vegetable oil

2 teaspoons vanilla extract

½ cup chopped walnuts

2 cups zucchini, grated

Preheat the oven to 350° F. Generously grease two 9 X 5-inch loaf pans. In a large bowl, mix the first 6 ingredients. Add the eggs, oil, vanilla, walnuts, and grated zucchini. Beat together until well blended. Pour the mixture equally into both loaf pans and bake for 1 hour. Serve warm with your meal or as a dessert.

Bette's Baked Crusty-Crumb Asparagus

Asparagus is another vegetable that can be hard to get kids to eat, but they seem to love it when it's prepared this way. One of the hardest of all of the vegetables to harvest, asparagus is great simply steamed, eaten raw with a little dip, or in this family-favorite recipe.

18-24 spears asparagus

6 tablespoons butter

1 small yellow onion, chopped

3 cloves garlic, chopped

2 tablespoons Italian parsley, chopped

Pinch of tarragon

2 cups bread crumbs

Preheat oven to 350° F. In a skillet of boiling water, gently put in asparagus and blanch. Drain the asparagus and place in a buttered shallow baking pan. In a skillet, melt the butter and sauté the onion, garlic, parsley, and tarragon. Add the bread crumbs and mix well. Spoon the bread crumb mixture over the asparagus and cover the pan with foil. Bake for 10-15 minutes. Remove the foil and bake at 400° F for an additional 5 minutes.

Bette's Best Cream of Broccoli Soup

One of Bette's best soups, cream of broccoli is hearty, flavorful, delicious, simple to make, and perfect for a rainy day; garnish it with cheese if you like.

Yields 4 servings

¼ cup unsalted or salted butter

¼ cup chopped onions

2 tablespoons flour

2 10¾-ounce cans chicken broth

1 cup heavy cream

1 cup half and half

¼ teaspoon salt

½ teaspoon ground black pepper

1 head broccoli, trimmed and chopped

Shredded cheddar cheese (optional)

In a large soup pot, melt the butter over moderate heat. Add the onions and sauté until translucent. Sprinkle in the flour and stir until the mixture has thickened. Add the chicken broth, heavy cream, half and half, salt, pepper, and broccoli and gently stir together. Cover and bring to a boil, stirring occasionally. Turn heat to low and simmer for an additional 15 minutes. Serve and sprinkle cheddar cheese on top of soup if desired.

Mama Louise's Lucky Leek & Potato Soup

Creamy leek and potato soup is a French classic that's quick, easy, and delicious to make. My mom made one of the best potato leek soups in the world and I still remember it vividly. As a quick tip, leeks are grown in sandy soil, so be sure to wash them really well – nobody wants sandy soup!

2 bunches leeks

6 medium-large potatoes

1 cup half and half

2-3 tablespoons butter

½ cup onion, chopped

1 quart chicken broth

1 teaspoon powdered garlic

Salt and pepper to taste

2 tablespoons fresh parsley, chopped

4 ounces cheddar cheese, shredded (optional)

Clean and chop leeks. Heat butter, add leeks and onion, and cook until tender. Add cubed potatoes and broth and cook until tender. Add half and half and simmer for 20 minutes more, adding seasonings and adjusting as necessary. Add parsley and cheddar cheese; stir and serve.

Bette's Easy Eggplant Parmigiana

Eggplant parmigiana is a true Italian classic and a longtime favorite in the Napolitano household. Here's a good tip, however – if you salt the eggplant first, it draws a lot of the moisture out of the eggplant and prevents the parmigiana from becoming soggy or watery while baking. Enjoy!

Prepared tomato sauce

2 large eggplants

Egg and milk mixture (roughly 3 eggs mixed with ½ cup milk for two large eggplants)

Vegetable or canola oil

Bread crumbs

1 pound mozzarella, shredded

1 cup Parmesan or Romano cheese

Salt to taste

Preheat oven to 350° F. Cut unpeeled eggplant lengthwise into slices about 1/8-¼-inch thick. Dip eggplant into egg and milk mixture, then into bread crumbs, both sides. In a large frying pan, heat oil until hot and fry eggplant until golden brown; drain on paper towels. In a large baking pan, place sauce on bottom of pan to cover and follow with a layer of eggplant slices. Then pour sauce over eggplant slices, sprinkle mozzarella cheese over the sauce, sprinkle Parmesan or Romano cheese, add a pinch of salt, and repeat the layers, ending with tomato sauce and mozzarella cheese on top. Bake for approximately 25 minutes.

Chef Bob's Iron Skillet Zucchini Rollup Lasagna

One great way to enjoy zucchini is in the following "lasagna" dish created by my good friend and orthopedist, Dr. Robert Doidge. It's very hearty and nutritious, serves 6-8 people, and always hits the mark for a hungry group!

7 medium-sized zucchini (local, farm-fresh ones if available)

8 ounces pancetta

1 medium red onion, chopped

1 cup shiitake mushrooms

1 cup button mushrooms

½ cup dry white wine

Red pepper flakes

Marinara sauce of your choice

Extra virgin olive oil

Ricotta, parmesan, and mozzarella cheese to taste

Parsley

Brown pancetta in a skillet and remove. Cook red onion and mushrooms in pan with a pinch of red pepper flakes to taste, then remove and deglaze with dry white wine. Return everything to the pan and add your favorite marinara to this base (Dr. Bob makes his own with San Marzano tomatoes, oil, and garlic sautéed lightly and simmered for 15-20 minutes).

Cut ends off of zucchini and slice thinly lengthwise using a knife or mandolin slicer (watch your fingers!). Place on a rack, salt, and let sit for 25 minutes, then wipe salt off and press down with cloth towel to remove excess water. Place zucchini slices in extra virgin olive oil to marinate, then grill zucchini over medium heat for approximately 6 minutes – only until tender, not grilled.

Coat a large iron skillet with a thin film of oil and a light layer of the sauce and roll zucchini slices with a light layer of ricotta, parsley, parmesan cheese, mozzarella cheese. and salt and pepper to create a gluten free, low-carb mock lasagna. Place in a 375-degree oven for approximately 20 minutes or until cheese is bubbly. Serve to friends and family with a loaf of fresh Italian bread and good wine, good music, and laughter!

Bette's Best Blueberry Muffins

Perfect for brunch or breakfast, homemade blueberry muffins are light, fluffy, packed with antioxidant-rich blueberries, and one of my family's all-time favorites. In the northeast, blueberries are plentiful (and their price is good) around the beginning of July, so be sure to get your fill!

2 cups unbleached all-purpose flour

2 teaspoons baking powder

¼ teaspoon fine salt

½ cup unsalted butter, softened, plus more for preparing the muffin tin

1 teaspoon finely grated lemon zest

2/3 cup sugar, plus 1 tablespoon for the top of the muffins (if desired)

2 large eggs, at room temperature

½ cup whole milk

1½ cups fresh blueberries, rinsed and dried

Preheat the oven to 375° F. Lightly brush a 12-muffin tin with butter and set aside. Sift the flour, baking powder, and salt into a medium bowl and set aside. In a standing mixer fitted with the paddle attachment or with an electric hand-held mixer in a large bowl, cream the butter, zest, and 2/3 cup of sugar until light and fluffy, about 2 minutes. Scrape down the sides of the bowl with a rubber spatula. Add the eggs, one at a time, beating well after each addition. Remove the bowl from the mixer. Using a rubber spatula, fold the flour in three parts into the butter mixture, alternating with the milk in two parts, until just combined. Fold in the blueberries. Take care not to overmix the batter. Divide the batter evenly into the muffin tin and sprinkle the tops with sugar (if desired). Bake until golden brown, about 25 minutes. Cool muffins in the pan on a rack. Serve warm.

Mrs. Johnson's Jersey Peach Pie

Whenever I see peaches, it always reminds me of my youth and the times when I would go up to Francis Johnson's peach farm in Ramsey, NJ with my father to pick up peaches so that we could sell them off the back of our truck. His wife, Mrs. Johnson, was often baking peach pies in the kitchen, so of course my younger brother David and I were always up for a great piece of pie. There's nothing better than fresh peach pie right out of the oven!

1 (15-ounce) package of pastry for a 9-inch double crust pie

1 egg, beaten

5 cups white and yellow Jersey peaches, sliced

2 tablespoons lemon juice

½ cup all-purpose flour

1 cup sugar

½ teaspoon ground cinnamon

¼ teaspoon ground nutmeg

¼ teaspoon salt

2 tablespoons butter

Preheat the oven to 450° F. Line the bottom and sides of a 9-inch pie plate with one of the pie crusts. Brush with some of the beaten egg to keep the dough from becoming soggy later. Place the sliced peaches in a large bowl, and sprinkle with lemon juice. Mix gently. In a separate bowl, mix together the flour, sugar, cinnamon, nutmeg, and salt. Pour over the peaches and mix gently. Pour into the pie crust and dot with butter. Cover with the other pie crust and fold the edges under. Flute the edges to seal or press the edges with the tines of a fork dipped in egg. Brush the remaining egg over the top crust. Cut several slits in the top crust to vent steam. Bake for 10 minutes in the preheated oven, then reduce the heat to 350° F and bake for an additional 30-35 minutes, until the crust is brown and the juice begins to bubble through the vents. If the edges brown too fast, cover them with strips of aluminum foil about halfway through baking. Cool a bit before serving, as this tastes better warm than hot.

Bette's Very Cherry Cheesecake

Cherries have one big flaw – their season is very short – so when they're available you want to get your fill. Every summer I ask Bette to make her cherry cheesecake because it's so delicious; while it's not necessarily good for my waistline, it's well worth the indulgence!

Crust

1¾ cups graham cracker crumbs

¼ cup chopped walnuts

2 teaspoons ground cinnamon

½ cup unsalted butter or margarine, melted

Filling

3 eggs

¼ teaspoon salt

1 pound cream cheese, at room temperature

1 cup sugar

2 teaspoons vanilla extract

1 teaspoon almond extract

3 cups sour cream

1½ cups fresh cherries, pitted and cut in half

Preheat the oven to 375° F. In a bowl, mix together all the crust ingredients, then press mixture on the bottom and sides of an 8 or 9-inch springform pan. In a large bowl, beat the eggs, salt, cream cheese, sugar, vanilla, and almond extract until smooth. Blend in the sour cream. Pour the filling into the prepared crust and bake for 35 minutes or until a knife inserted into the center comes out clean. Top with cherries, chill for 3 hours, and enjoy!

Bette's Brilliant Lemon (or Orange) Cake

Fresh lemon or orange – you can absolutely replace the lemon with fresh orange for a great orange cake – totally make this cake, which is one of the most popular items our friends ask Bette to make. It's not necessarily fancy to look at, but its signature taste makes everyone beg for more.

½ pound (2 sticks) butter

3 cups all-purpose flour

3 cups sugar (or less to taste)

1 cup sour cream

½ teaspoon baking soda

6 eggs

1 teaspoon lemon extract

Lemon rind of one lemon, grated

3 tablespoons fresh lemon juice

<u>Icing</u>

1½ cups confectioner's sugar, or less to taste

Fresh lemon juice to taste

1 tablespoon lemon rind, grated

Preheat the oven to 325° F. Butter and flour a tube pan and set aside. In a large bowl, cream butter and sugar together and then add sour cream. Sift flour and baking soda together. Add to creamed mixture, alternately with eggs, one at a time, beating after each addition. Add lemon extract, lemon rind, and lemon juice and stir to combine. Pour into prepared pan and bake for 1 hour and 10 minutes. Cool cake in pan for about 10 minutes and then unmold and cool completely on a wire rack. Mix icing ingredients together with a whisk until they take on a thick, liquid consistency; drizzle icing over cake when it's still warm.

Bette's Famous Butternut Squash Ravioli with Sage Butter Sauce

This a great recipe that's traditionally made in our house at Thanksgiving or Christmas (when butternut squash is in season), but it's so good you can make it anytime!

1 large butternut squash, halved lengthwise, peeled, and seeded

2 teaspoons butter

Salt and ground black pepper to taste

½ teaspoon allspice

½ teaspoon ground nutmeg

2 teaspoons ground cinnamon

½ cup Parmesan cheese

Pre-made/store-bought ravioli sheets or wonton wraps

Sage Butter Sauce

1 teaspoon cornstarch

1 tablespoon cold water

1 cup chicken broth

2 teaspoons dried sage

3 tablespoons butter, cut in pieces, melted

Preheat oven to 350° F. Place the squash cut side up on a baking sheet. Place 1 tablespoon butter in the hollow of each half. Sprinkle with salt and pepper to taste. Cover the squash with a sheet of aluminum foil, tucking in the edges. Bake squash in preheated oven until tender and easily pierced with a fork, 45-65 minutes. Scoop the cooked squash into a bowl and mash until smooth. Mix in the allspice, nutmeg, cinnamon, and Parmesan cheese until well-blended. Season to taste with salt and pepper.

To Make the Sage Butter Sauce: In small bowl, blend cornstarch with cold water. In a 10-inch skillet, heat chicken broth over high heat and cook 3 minutes or until slightly reduced. Add dried sage and cornstarch mixture and boil 1 minute.

Remove pan from heat, swirl in butter until melted, and pour over ravioli.

Fill ravioli sheets or wonton wrappers with a spoonful of butternut squash mixture to taste, pinch them closed, bake or boil ravioli per package directions, and serve with sage butter sauce.

CHAPTER 14

LOOKING BACK...AND AHEAD

When my kids were growing up, I worked all the time and made excuses for not being there for their athletic games, school events, and other milestones. When my grandkids came along, they were my second chance.

My daughter Cheryl, who's an accountant and lives a few minutes away from us, has three kids – twins Alexandra and Zachary (whom fans might recall were preemies and looked no bigger than yams when they were born – they're great now!) and younger sister Gabriella. My son Peter, who was a receiver for a large food company for many years after we sold our store and continues to work in the produce industry, has four kids – sons Nicholas, Griffin, and Jake and daughter Jaedyn. Bette and I have been extremely involved in their lives, attending all of their special events and games (at least for those kids who live near us), and I talk to all of them about life, values, and the importance of being kind, being careful about the things they say and do, and being respectful of others. I remember one time I got up and walked out of a restaurant because they wouldn't put their phones down; we're a talking family and I want to spend quality time with them.

Christmas with our seven grandkids years ago

My grandchildren are great kids and they're the absolute loves of my and Bette's ("Nanny's") life; however, like many young people, they don't necessarily understand or appreciate what my life was like when I was their age or how precious and scarce money and material things were for us. Years ago, my granddaughter Alexandra famously laughed and rolled her eyes at me when I told her how excited my brother and I were to receive oranges in our Christmas stockings as kids. *"Really*, Poppy???" she said. My grandkids have only ever known me as Produce Pete – not as anyone else or someone who did anything else before that – and they think nothing of people coming up to us on the street or in a restaurant to ask for a picture with me because it's second nature to them.

172

Aside from my weekly segments on WNBC *Weekend Today in New York* and my part-time work for S. Katzman Produce, I speak to school kids throughout New Jersey about 10 times a year (pre-pandemic) – mostly 4th-8th graders, but some high school and college students as well. With an emphasis on keeping things light and making them laugh, I speak to them about produce, my life as a peddler, and how I knew from a very young age that I'd either go to work or go across the street and rob a bank. I talk to them about farms, why apples and oranges are good for them, and how to pick them and they really latch on to my tips. When I started working with Pathmark in the early 2000s, that company arranged for me to make a lot of appearances at schools to help nurture the next generation, but now I happily do it on my own nickel to help give back, and I find it very rewarding.

Speaking to elementary school students about the importance of eating fruits and vegetables

From June through October (except during the pandemic), I've also typically made appearances at a lot of farmer's markets, festivals, and health fairs around New Jersey. In the beginning, I just went to these events and shook hands; it's since evolved into demonstrations, selling and signing books, aprons, and bags, and taking pictures. I love meeting people and feel so honored and grateful that they come out to see me and enjoy hearing what I have to say.

In the over 30 years that I've been with WNBC, I've only missed my on-air segments maybe two or three times due to sickness. I've always had a bad stomach and suffered a bout of diverticulitis years ago, but around the time I turned 50, things got worse and I was diagnosed with Crohn's disease. It took me several different doctors and a lot of trial and error with medication and diet to get it under control, but I'm happy to say that I seem to have landed on a good protocol and am effectively managing the condition. Every few weeks I get a several-hour infusion of a drug which helps to tamp down the inflammation associated with Crohn's disease and it's worked pretty well for me so far. Though I sometimes get a little tired and out of sorts right after each infusion, these side effects are very tolerable and I've learned to live with and work around them because I know that there are a lot of worse things out there.

I've witnessed a lot of things in my lifetime, but in my nearly eight decades I must say that I've never experienced anything like the COVID-19 pandemic, which materially changed life and upended the economy like nothing I've ever seen. I ended up doing my segments in the WNBC studio on March 7th and

March 14th, 2020, but with all of the fear and uncertainty swirling around the coronavirus as well as the mounting number of cases in New York City during that month, the executives at WNBC asked me what I'd be comfortable doing. I told them that in light of my age and compromised immune system, I'd refrain from coming into the studio for a while and would return when the virus cleared out. News anchors Pat Battle and Gus Rosendale started doing the Saturday morning broadcasts from their homes too and only a skeleton crew remained in the studio to minimize the number of people in the building. I also stopped going to the S. Katzman Produce offices at the Hunts Point Market, which similarly pared down its staff to a skeleton crew to help reduce the risk of transmitting or contracting COVID.

Though I started working for S. Katzman Produce from home in the middle of March, I didn't plan on doing any of my WNBC segments from home; like so many other people, I never expected that the public health crisis we were dealing with would last that long and I just figured I'd take a short hiatus from the show. I remember watching TV in March and seeing spring breakers in Florida living it up on the beach like nothing was happening and thinking how funny it was that when you're young you never think you're going to die and when you're old you think you're going to die the next day!

About a week into my "hiatus," I thought I'd do a little video from my kitchen thanking the doctors, nurses, farmers, delivery drivers, food workers, and other front-line heroes who were working so hard for others during this scary, challenging, and unprecedented time. I posted the footage on my Twitter and Facebook accounts and after seeing it, my producer asked whether I'd be willing to do a segment for WNBC *Weekend Today in New York* from my kitchen once a week – just like old times, except from my home. The footage went over well with viewers and for the rest of that year and all throughout 2021 and 2022 – so far – I've done a weekly segment from our kitchen table, living room couch, or outdoor patio covering everything from asparagus and apples to tomatoes, Brussels sprouts, persimmons, potatoes, pears, and more, including some field segments at Farms View in Wayne and Donaldson's Farm in Hackettstown in the warm-weather months. I've been excited to continue connecting with viewers to share information on seasonal produce and new recipes from the safety of my home during a two-year period like no other.

The pandemic created devastating ripple effects throughout the entire food industry, with farmers, wholesalers, and grocery stores alike experiencing everything from oversupplies to shortages and all of the price volatility associated with those situations; while some farmers had to throw out perishable product or sell it off at below-cost levels so that it wouldn't rot and be a complete waste, many Americans stood on lines for hours to receive supplemental food to feed their families. The unfortunate disconnects and inequities that surfaced throughout different parts of the country were apparent and it seemed that everyone felt the burn.

Doing weekly segments for NBC from my kitchen and patio during the pandemic

Like so many Americans, especially those of senior age, my once-standard routine changed materially. Bette and I vigilantly adhered to safety protocols like masking, social distancing, and hand-washing and we limited our activities outside the home to just necessities like grocery shopping, doctor's appointments, etc. As much as we love our kids and grandkids, we resorted mostly to Zoom calls with them instead of in-person visits and significantly reduced the number of people around our holiday table at Thanksgiving and Christmas. I also cancelled all of my previously-scheduled in-person appearances at schools, festivals, and health fairs.

While many people around me rebelled against the "new normal," I've taken it more in stride. I've acquired a greater level of patience over the years and know that we'll eventually be out of the woods and that things will eventually even out. My message throughout the heart of the pandemic was "stay home, stay safe," and I'm just grateful to be here. Both Bette and I completed the COVID vaccination process in early 2021 and received the boosters that became available later in 2021 and 2022 and we look forward to the promise of brighter days and a return to normalcy soon!

If you asked me years ago, I can honestly say that I thought I'd be president of the United States before I'd ever be on TV. I attribute a lot of what happened to me and my longevity on TV to luck, and maybe some "happy accidents" and fortuitous decisions. You can make a right turn at the corner and find a pot of gold or get hit by a car – I guess it's about making the right decision at the right time, knowing when to recognize and take advantage of an opportunity that's presented to you, and being on the receiving end of some old-fashioned good luck.

Doing a recent field segment on Jersey tomatoes at Farms View in Wayne, NJ for NBC 4 New York's Weekend Today in New York

I remember that, as a little kid growing up in a poor, post-WWII household trying to sell tomatoes or apples door-to-door, you only had a few seconds before the homeowner shut the door in your face, so you had to be cute or funny. I went for both. I'd say something to them like, "feel sorry for me, lady – my dad might make me walk home!" and see something in their face instantly soften and connect with me on a human level. In many ways, being on TV has felt very natural for me because it's been like going home to the place I started over 70 years ago.

While I may have become an expert on produce based on the hard-won, first-hand knowledge I've amassed over seven decades in the industry, believe it or not, more people want to hear about my life than anything else. They love the stories and recipes that have emanated from a colorful past filled with an unforgettable mosaic of people and life experiences that are indelibly emblazoned on my heart. As a kid, I peddled at homes where Buddy Hackett and Tony Bennett answered the door and counted everyone from hard-working local families to baseball legends Yogi Berra and Elston Howard and singer Ben E. King as loyal customers of our store. I married my high school/"forever" sweetheart, had two fantastic kids and seven wonderful grandkids, and ran a successful, second-generation business that was a mainstay in town for nearly half a century. I've had weekly segments on major TV networks for over 30 years, spoke at the Harvard Club where JFK and Dwight D. Eisenhower had once spoken (I remember asking the contact who invited me, "are you sure you have the right guy?!"), and recently threw out the first pitch at a local baseball game alongside New York Yankees All-Star and Cy Young Award-winning pitcher Sparky Lyle. Wonders never cease!

Me with legendary New York Yankees pitcher Sparky Lyle
(I'm a huge fan!) at a Somerset Patriots baseball game in Bridgewater, NJ

There have certainly been some ups and downs in my life along the way, but all in all, I consider myself one lucky guy. I like to believe that I've always been true to myself, avoiding situations that made me feel obligated to something or someone and turning down jobs that didn't fit or feel right. At the heart of it all, I think that some of my longevity in the media world comes from sincerely liking people. If I wasn't doing TV, I think I'd be sitting on a park bench watching people – their actions, interactions, dynamics, and expressions are endlessly fascinating to me. I also think that it isn't hard to be nice. When people take the time out of their day to stand in line to say hello to me or take a picture, it's the biggest compliment in the world, especially for a guy like me.

There isn't an item I cover on TV that doesn't bring back a host of memories. The smells, the sights – our lives always revolved around the kitchen. For me, it all comes down to family. Though we may have disagreements sometimes, I'd never be the person I am without my childhood or my mom and dad, siblings, Bette, and our family.

Bette and I have a really good life today, but if it all went away, I wouldn't be jumping off a roof. All of the luxuries and creature comforts in life won't necessarily make you happy or keep you in a marriage; they're just a tool, because true happiness comes from within. Despite my tough upbringing, I never look back on any of it in anger because everything that happened brought me to where I am today; I feel proud of where I came from and the experiences I had because they made me who I am. It's become so easy to do anything today – get a divorce if you don't get along, quit a job if you don't like the terms or your co-workers, change schools if you don't like the environment – but I never took the easy way out of anything. As my story demonstrates, real life isn't always easy, but the satisfaction of working hard and facing challenges head-on has brought me a sense of peace and accomplishment that no shortcut or quick fix could ever deliver. It even led to a lucky break on TV!

Me and Bette, my "forever girl," during a field segment at
Donaldson's Farm in Hackettstown, NJ in 2018

On that note, I'm grateful for my beloved family members and friends, the wonderful colleagues who believed and saw something in me that I never would have on my own, and the incredible fans who have tuned in and shared their love, support, and stories for over three decades and helped make one guy's life-long dream come true.

At a recent family event with my sister LuAnne and brother David

*Enjoying food and memories with Bette and our extended
family during my son Peter's 50th birthday celebration*

Finally, I'm especially grateful for the universal and continuous life thread that seems to connect us all – food and memories. I hope that this trip down memory lane with me helps inspire your own good memories – past, present, and future.

About the Authors

With over 70 years of experience in the produce industry, renowned fruit and vegetable expert, author, and TV personality **"Produce Pete" Napolitano** has appeared on a highly-popular segment on NBC's *Weekend Today in New York* broadcast every Saturday morning for 30 years. *They Call Me Produce Pete* is the long-awaited follow-up to his first book, *Produce Pete's Farmacopeia*.

Susan Bloom is an award-winning writer whose work has appeared in such New Jersey-based publications as *The Star-Ledger, The Asbury Park Press, New Jersey Monthly Magazine*, and *Jersey's Best Magazine* as well as such national mediums as *USA Today, The New York Daily News*, and *Natural Awakenings*. She's collaborated with Produce Pete on a broad range of articles and monthly columns for over a decade.

CPSIA information can be obtained
at www.ICGtesting.com
Printed in the USA
BVHW042301090223
658260BV00006B/203